AMERICAN THEORISTS
OF THE NOVEL

The American theorists Henry James, Lionel Trilling, and Wayne C. Booth have revolutionized our understanding of narrative or story-telling, and have each championed the novel as an art form. Concepts from their work have become part of the fabric of novel criticism today, influencing theorists, authors, and readers alike.

Emphasizing the crucial relationship between the work of these three critics, Peter Rawlings explores their understanding of the novel form, and investigates their ideas on:

- realism and representation
- authors and narration
- point of view and centres of consciousness
- readers, reading, and interpretation
- moral intelligence.

Rawlings demonstrates the importance of James, Trilling, and Booth for contemporary literary theory and clearly introduces critical concepts that underlie any study of narrative. This book is invaluable reading for anyone with an interest in American critical theory, or the genre of the novel.

Peter Rawlings is Reader in English and American Literature and Head of English and Drama at the University of the West of England, Bristol (UK). He has published widely on Henry James, American theories of fiction in the nineteenth century, and the American reception of Shakespeare.

ROUTLEDGE CRITICAL THINKERS

Series Editor: Robert Eaglestone, Royal Holloway, University of London

Routledge Critical Thinkers is a series of accessible introductions to key figures in contemporary critical thought.

With a unique focus on historical and intellectual contexts, the volumes in this series examine important theorists':

* significance
* motivation
* key ideas and their sources
* impact on other thinkers

Concluding with extensively annotated guides to further reading, *Routledge Critical Thinkers* are the student's passport to today's most exciting critical thought.

Already available:

Louis Althusser by Luke Ferretter
Roland Barthes by Graham Allen
Jean Baudrillard by Richard J. Lane
Simone de Beauvoir by Ursula Tidd
Homi K. Bhabha by David Huddart
Maurice Blanchot by Ullrich Haase and William Large
Judith Butler by Sara Salih
Gilles Deleuze by Claire Colebrook
Jacques Derrida by Nicholas Royle
Michel Foucault by Sara Mills
Sigmund Freud by Pamela Thurschwell
Stuart Hall by James Procter
Martin Heidegger by Timothy Clark
Fredric Jameson by Adam Roberts
Jacques Lacan by Sean Homer
Julia Kristeva by Noëlle McAfee

Jean-François Lyotard by Simon Malpas
Paul de Man by Martin McQuillan
Friedrich Nietzsche by Lee Spinks
Paul Ricoeur by Karl Simms
Edward Said by Bill Ashcroft and Pal Ahluwalia
Gayatri Chakravorty Spivak by Stephen Morton
Slavoj Žižek by Tony Myers
Theorists of the Modernist Novel: James Joyce, Dorothy Richardson, and Virginia Woolf by Deborah Parsons
Theorists of Modernist Poetry: T. S. Eliot, T. E. Hulme, and Ezra Pound by Rebecca Beasley

For further details on this series, see www.routledge.com/literature/series.asp

AMERICAN THEORISTS OF THE NOVEL

HENRY JAMES,
LIONEL TRILLING,
WAYNE C. BOOTH

Peter Rawlings

Routledge
Taylor & Francis Group

LONDON AND NEW YORK

First published 2006
by Routledge
2 Park Square, Milton Park, Abingdon, Oxon OX14 4RN

Simultaneously published in the USA and Canada
by Routledge
270 Madison Avenue, New York, NY 10016

Routledge is an imprint of the Taylor & Francis Group, an informa business

© 2006 Peter Rawlings

Typeset in Perpetua by
Florence Production Ltd, Stoodleigh, Devon
Printed and bound in Great Britain by
TJ International Ltd, Padstow, Cornwall

British Library Cataloguing in Publication Data
A catalogue record for this book is available from
the British Library

Library of Congress Cataloging in Publication Data
Rawlings, Peter.
    American theorists of the novel: Henry James, Lionel Trilling,
and Wayne C. Booth/Peter Rawlings.
        p. cm. – (Routledge critical thinkers)
    Includes bibliographical references and index.
    1. Criticism–United States. 2. Fiction–History and criticism.
    I. Title. II. Series.
    PN99.U52R39 2006
    808.3–dc22   2005036198

ISBN10: 0–415–28544–5 (hbk)
ISBN10: 0–415–28545–3 (pbk)
ISBN10: 0–203–96947–2 (ebk)

ISBN13: 978–0–415–28544–5 (hbk)
ISBN13: 978–0–415–28545–2 (pbk)
ISBN13: 978–0–203–96947–2 (ebk)

SUCH AS IT IS,
IN MEMORY OF WAYNE C. BOOTH
(1921–2005)

CONTENTS

SERIES EDITOR'S PREFACE

The books in this series offer introductions to major critical thinkers who have influenced literary studies and the humanities. The *Routledge Critical Thinkers* series provides the books you can turn to first when a new name or concept appears in your studies.

Each book will equip you to approach these thinkers' original texts by explaining their key ideas, putting them into context and, perhaps most importantly, showing you why they are considered to be significant. The emphasis is on concise, clearly written guides that do not presuppose a specialist knowledge. Although the focus is on particular figures, the series stresses that no critical thinker ever existed in a vacuum but, instead, emerged from a broader intellectual, cultural and social history. Finally, these books will act as a bridge between you and their original texts: not replacing them but, rather, complementing what they wrote. In some cases, volumes consider small clusters of thinkers working in the same area, developing similar ideas or influencing each other.

These books are necessary for a number of reasons. In his 1997 autobiography, *Not Entitled*, the literary critic Frank Kermode wrote of a time in the 1960s:

On beautiful summer lawns, young people lay together all night, recovering from their daytime exertions and listening to a troupe of Balinese musicians.

> Under their blankets or their sleeping bags, they would chat drowsily about
> the gurus of the time ... What they repeated was largely hearsay; hence my
> lunchtime suggestion, quite impromptu, for a series of short, very cheap books
> offering authoritative but intelligible introductions to such figures.

There is still a need for 'authoritative and intelligible introductions', but this series reflects a different world from the 1960s. New thinkers have emerged and the reputations of others have risen and fallen, as new research has developed. New methodologies and challenging ideas have spread through the arts and humanities. The study of literature is no longer – if it ever was – simply the study and evaluation of poems, novels, and plays. It is also the study of the ideas, issues, and difficulties which arise in any literary text and in its interpretation. Other arts and humanities subjects have changed in analogous ways.

With these changes, new problems have emerged. The ideas and issues behind these radical changes in the humanities are often presented without reference to wider contexts or as theories that you can simply 'add on' to the texts you read. Certainly, there's nothing wrong with picking out selected ideas or using what comes to hand – indeed, some thinkers have argued that this is, in fact, all we can do. However, it is sometimes forgotten that each new idea comes from the pattern and development of somebody's thought and it is important to study the range and context of their ideas. Against theories 'floating in space', the *Routledge Critical Thinkers* series places key thinkers and their ideas firmly back in their contexts.

More than this, these books reflect the need to go back to the thinkers' own texts and ideas. Every interpretation of an idea, even the most seemingly innocent one, offers its own 'spin', implicitly or explicitly. To read only books on a thinker, rather than texts by that thinker, is to deny yourself a chance of making up your own mind. Sometimes what makes a significant figure's work hard to approach is not so much its style or content as the feeling of not knowing where to start. The purpose of these books is to give you a 'way in' by offering an accessible overview of these thinkers' ideas and works and by guiding your further reading, starting with each thinker's own texts. To use a metaphor from the philosopher Ludwig Wittgenstein (1889–1951), these books are ladders, to be thrown away after you have climbed to the next level. Not only, then, do they equip you to approach new ideas, but also they empower you, by leading you back to a theorist's own texts and encouraging you to develop your own informed opinions.

Finally, these books are necessary because, just as intellectual needs have changed, the education systems around the world – the contexts in which introductory books are usually read – have changed radically, too. What was suitable for the minority higher education system of the 1960s is not suitable for the larger, wider, more diverse, high technology education systems of the twenty-first century. These changes call not just for new, up-to-date introductions but new methods of presentation. The presentational aspects of *Routledge Critical Thinkers* have been developed with today's students in mind.

Each book in the series has a similar structure. They begin with a section offering an overview of the life and ideas of the featured thinkers and explaining why they are important. The central section of the books discusses the thinkers' key ideas, their context, evolution and reception: with the books that deal with more than one thinker, they also explain and explore the influence of each on each. The volumes conclude with a survey of the impact of the thinker or thinkers, outlining how their ideas have been taken up and developed by others. In addition, there is a detailed final section suggesting and describing books for further reading. This is not a 'tacked-on' section but an integral part of each volume. In the first part of this section you will find brief descriptions of the key works by the featured thinkers; then, following this, information on the most useful critical works and, in some cases, on relevant websites. This section will guide you in your reading, enabling you to follow your interests and develop your own projects. Throughout each book, references are given in what is known as the Harvard system (the author and the date of a work cited are given in the text and you can look up the full details in the bibliography at the back). This offers a lot of information in very little space. The books also explain technical terms and use boxes to describe events or ideas in more detail, away from the main emphasis of the discussion. Boxes are also used at times to highlight definitions of terms frequently used or coined by a thinker. In this way, the boxes serve as a kind of glossary, easily identified when flicking through the book.

The thinkers in the series are 'critical' for three reasons. First, they are examined in the light of subjects that involve criticism: principally, literary, studies or English and cultural studies, but also other disciplines that rely on the criticism of books, ideas, theories and unquestioned assumptions. Second, they are critical because studying their work will provide you with a 'tool kit' for your own informed critical reading and thought, which will make you critical. Third, these thinkers are critical because they are crucially important: they deal with ideas and questions that can overturn conventional understandings of the world, of texts, of everything we take for granted, leaving us with a deeper understanding of what we already knew and with new ideas.

No introduction can tell you everything. However, by offering a way into critical thinking, this series hopes to begin to engage you in an activity which is productive, constructive, and potentially life-changing.

WHY JAMES, TRILLING, AND BOOTH?

Why read James, Trilling, and Booth? The answer may not be immediately obvious. Writing from the 1860s and through to the early twentieth century, Henry James (1843–1916) is most widely renowned for works such as *The Wings of the Dove* (1902b), *The Golden Bowl* (1904), *The Portrait of a Lady* (1881), and his ghost story, 'The Turn of the Screw' (1898). But he also published ground-breaking prefaces to his own fiction and numerous critical essays. Lionel Trilling (1905–75) became well known as a literary critic in a 1950s academic scene dominated by, as we shall see, the 'New Criticism' of earlier decades. The academic career of Wayne C. Booth (1921–2005), on the other hand, has spanned the later twentieth-century transformation of literary 'criticism' into the myriad new approaches known as literary 'theory'.

So why read the texts of these three American critics, and why read them alongside one another? Because the landmark works of James, Trilling, and Booth have in just over a century revolutionized our understanding of what narrative, or story-telling is, and how prose fiction (novels and stories) functions. They are among the most widely cited theorists of the novel, and their work has had an enormous influence on the writing, reading, and criticism of fiction. Read by academics and the general reader alike, Trilling's *The Liberal Imagination* (1950) was a bestseller in the US and soon had a huge impact on

NEW CRITICISM

The focus of New Criticism is on literature itself and away from the lives and times (the context) of particular writers. The text is regarded as self-sufficient; and the task is to subject it to 'close reading'. In 'The Intentional Fallacy' (1946) and 'The Affective Fallacy' (1949), W. K. Wimsatt and Monroe C. Beardsley argued that neither the author's intention nor the reader's feelings were relevant to interpreting and judging works of literature. This movement held sway for much of the twentieth century. Although the New Historicism of Stephen Greenblatt and others has redirected attention to correspondences between texts and history, it remains unfashionable in many quarters to use biographical material to interpret literary texts.

critical thinking internationally. It has gone through many editions subsequently. Together with the rest of Trilling's work, *The Liberal Imagination* is attracting attention again now that literary theory has lost much of the ground it took in the later twentieth century (some critics refer to the current period as 'post-theory'). James's essays, and especially his prefaces to the New York edition of his work, continue to be a dominant force in discussions about fiction. Booth's *The Rhetoric of Fiction* has been indispensable to students of the novel ever since its first publication in 1961. Concepts from their work have become part of the fabric of novel criticism today: we have James's ideas on 'points of view' and 'centres of consciousness', Trilling's 'moral realism' and 'the liberal imagination', and Booth's 'implied author' and 'reliable/unreliable narration', to name but a few.

Their work has also had a huge effect on the status of the novel. In 1817, the Romantic poet and critic, Samuel Taylor Coleridge, was able to dismiss the reading of novels as a 'kill-time' rather than a 'pass-time', a 'species of *amusement*' akin to 'spitting over a bridge' (1817: 1: 34). Moreover, even at the end of a nineteenth century which had seen the achievements of novelists, (among many others) of Walter Scott, Charles Dickens, George Eliot, Gustave Flaubert, Ivan Turgenev, Leo Tolstoy, and Henry James himself, the minor American critic, George Clarke, was still comparing the effects of novel-reading with 'those of indulgence in opium and intoxicating liquors' (Clarke

1898: 362). At best, then, the novel was seen as a frivolous entertainment, and at worst, an immoral distraction from the practical world. Today, however, the novel is considered by a majority of critics to be a flexible form of art uniquely suited to the inspection of individual, social, and moral health. It has, as Trilling put it in *The Liberal Imagination,* a 'reconstitutive and renovating power' (1950: 253). To understand this new perspective, and the work from which it emerged, it is essential to engage with the writings of Henry James, Lionel Trilling, and Wayne C. Booth. This book provides a guide to their major work on theories of the novel and a companion for your own reading of the key texts.

DIFFERENT CONTEXTS, COMMON CONCERNS

Although the work of these three critics emerges from varied contexts, all three share a preoccupation with a set of ethical and moral questions about fiction that subsequent critics have been unable to ignore. Is it possible to have 'good' novels about 'bad' people? Should it be the function of the novel to make the reader a 'better', more socially responsible person? Do we, in any event, have common standards by which to assess such improvements? Should a novelist pass clear judgements on his characters? Is it morally dangerous for authors to multiply ambiguities or uncertainties about meaning?

The ethics of reading and writing and the moral consequences of formal and technical decisions are central concerns for these critics and, as a result of their influence, for theorists of the novel in general. On the basis of even a cursory glance at these concerns it is clear that James, Trilling, and Booth focus not only on what texts *are*, but also on *how they are put together*, or on what it is about their organization in language that makes them tick. In varying degrees, they are all interested in these matters of content, form, and technique; but they are even more preoccupied with what texts can *do*, with how they hook on to the world, and with the impact they can have on readers. As Trilling memorably expresses it, literary structures are not 'static and commemorative but mobile and aggressive, and one does not describe a quinquereme or a howitzer or a tank without estimating how much *damage* it can do' (1965: 11).

For these critics, communication, for good or for ill, is at the centre of the business of reading, writing, and grasping novels critically.

ETHICS AND MORALS

'Ethics' are the rules that regulate our behaviour in specific practical areas (such as medicine or literary criticism). 'Morals' are the underlying principles shaping these ethics.

Wayne Booth, the last in this theoretical genealogy, constructed a model of the communication process, making explicit many of the concepts that had been implicit in the work of the others. I shall turn to Booth's model shortly, as a slightly modified version of it provides the structure for this guide. At this point, however, we might consider a little more closely the lives and contexts of each of our three critics. As this guide examines aspects of their work, I shall necessarily return to the particular 'hooks' between the critics' own texts and their worlds, but it may be useful to set the scene with some background information, to which you might easily return later.

HENRY JAMES (1843–1916)

The American republic was less than seventy years old when Henry James was born in Greenwich Village, New York City, in 1843. By 1864, the family had settled in Boston, Massachusetts, after more than twenty years of moving between America and Europe. The family was of Irish and Scottish descent. Henry James's grandfather had made a considerable fortune in business, but the shrinking inheritance had eventually to be divided, in Henry's generation, between five children. For these five, then, there was no prospect of the life without work that had been enjoyed by their father, a devotee of the Swedish mystic, Emanuel Swedenborg (1688–1772). Henry's father had a relaxed, even rather a scattered, approach to child-rearing. As befitted a man whose youth had been somewhat dissipated, his emphasis was on 'being' rather than 'doing', and this resulted in a certain shiftlessness in his children. After dabbling in painting for a while, Henry's older brother, William James (1842–1910), became an eminent psychologist and philosopher and, as we shall see in Chapter 4, exercised a significant impact on James's theory and practice of fiction. Henry himself studied law at Harvard, fitfully, before turning in earnest to the writing of fiction.

Despite the influence of American writers on his fiction and criticism – especially that of Nathaniel Hawthorne (1804–64), an author most widely known today for his romance, *The Scarlet Letter* (1850) – James's attachment was to the culture of Europe, to the Old World rather than the New. In his 1879 book, *Hawthorne*, James protested that America lacked the 'complex social machinery' necessary to 'set a writer in motion' (1879: 320). After his unlikely year at Harvard (1862–3) and further trips to Europe, he settled in England in 1876, twelve years after the appearance of his first reviews and fiction. He returned to America only occasionally, and became a naturalized British citizen shortly before his death in 1916. Apart from *Hawthorne*, a series of prefaces to the New York edition of his fiction (1907–9), and the numerous reviews and essays he never collected, James produced four volumes of literary criticism and theory: *French Poets and Novelists* (1878), *Partial Portraits* (1888b), *Essays in London and Elsewhere* (1893a), and *Notes on Novelists* (1914). Most of this material had been published previously in journals such as the *Atlantic Monthly* and the *Nation*. James was a prolific writer of fiction as well as a critic: there are twenty-two novels (two were unfinished) and over a hundred short stories (and some are not so short). He also wrote a number of very bad and spectacularly unsuccessful plays such as *Guy Domville* (1894).

From his youth on, James read widely in the English and European novel traditions. His fiction and criticism attempt to reconcile the social and moral intensities of English novelists such as George Eliot (1819–80) with the formal self-consciousness of French writers who often seemed to disregard morality. French authors especially important to James were Honoré de Balzac (1799–1850), Gustave Flaubert (1821–80), and Émile Zola (1840–1902). When James started writing fiction in the 1860s, novels were tolerated by a good many influential reviewers only if they were heavily didactic; if they aimed, that is, to teach moral lessons. The legacy of Puritanism in America meant that the theme of adultery, which was especially prominent in the French novel, was often beyond the pale of what was acceptable there for most readers, critics, and writers. When the American writer Nathaniel Hawthorne (1804–64) tackled this theme in *The Scarlet Letter* (1850), it was described by one reviewer as having a 'running underside of filth' (Coxe 1851: 489). James found himself caught between admiring the technique, or what he considered the *art*, of many French

PURITANISM

The Puritans arose as a party within the Church of England during the Reformation, the Protestant rebellion against Catholicism, in the sixteenth and early seventeenth centuries. They were opposed to what they saw as the excessive ceremonies and rituals of the newly established Church of England and supported parliamentary government, rather than the monarchy, at the time of the English Civil War and its aftermath (1640–60). Puritans made up the majority of early European settlers in New England (America) in the early seventeenth century. The label 'Puritanism' became associated with strict and oppressively uncompromising moral attitudes.

novelists and condemning, with increasing reluctance, their 'off-limits' subject-matter.

The title of Henry James's major critical essay, 'The Art of Fiction' (1884), makes it clear that he considered the writing of novels and short stories as an art in its own right, and it is hard to imagine just how challenging this view was at the time. When James began to write, fiction was often regarded as dubious by narrow moralists because it tended towards the projection of escapist worlds of romance and fantasy. But as we have seen, writers who attempted to write more realistically by including glimpses of the adult bedroom (for example) were frequently condemned outright. James soon became known as a realist in two related senses. First, he dealt with the recognizable world of everyday reality, or at least the cultivated segment of it with which he was familiar. Second, he tackled morally complex situations in which the rules of conduct adhered to by conservative readers were unlikely to be universally helpful.

James was pulled in two directions: the morally intense world of his American context (especially that of Boston, with those powerful residues of Puritanism, in which he began to write), and the (mainly French) world of art with its increasing devotion to form and technique at the expense of morality and moralizing. The pressure in America and also in Britain, where James took up residence, was to produce a filtered version of reality, an ideal world full of messages promoting self-improvement. In France, the growing enthusiasm was for the representation of the world in all its lurid reality. Embedded here is a deeper anxiety – and one set to continue in the Trilling and Booth eras, and beyond – about the perils of artful theory as distinct from the easy securities of artless moralizing.

The Russian writer Ivan Turgenev spent a good deal of time in France. Indeed, James included him in his *French Poets and Novelists*. In the 'moral beauty' (1896b: 1033) of his fiction – he called Turgenev the 'novelists' novelist' (1896b: 1029) – James saw an ideal balance between moral and aesthetic demands. Partly under Turgenev's influence, but also under that of the English critic and poet Matthew Arnold (1822–88) and that of Charles Augustin Sainte-Beuve (1804–69), the most significant French critic of his generation, James began to move to the idea in the 1880s that good art cannot but be moral. His sense of morality, however, was much closer to what was to become Trilling's 'moral realism' than to the conventional, rule-bound, environment of moral thinking in which his early criticism struggled to develop.

LIONEL TRILLING (1905–75)

Lionel Trilling's early ambition was to be a writer of fiction. Despite managing to produce only one novel, *The Middle of the Journey* (1947), and a number of short stories (the most successful of which, 'Of This Time, of That Place', appeared in 1943), he insisted late in life that 'being a critic' was not 'part of the plan' (1971: 227). Trilling, born, like James, in New York City, was the son of Jewish immigrant parents. He entered Columbia College, Columbia University (New York) as an undergraduate student in 1921. With the exception of some early teaching at the University of Wisconsin (Madison) and Hunter College (City University of New York) shortly after receiving his MA in 1926, he remained at Columbia until his death. He was the first Jew to be appointed to a regular, full-time position in an American university. Trilling shared James's enthusiasm for Matthew Arnold: his doctoral dissertation, which he had laboured over for most of the 1930s, and which was criticized by one examiner for being too readable, was published as *Matthew Arnold* in 1939. It was followed in 1943 by *E. M. Forster*, where the concept of 'moral realism' (to which we shall return in Chapter 6) was first developed. Trilling was as much a cultural critic as a theorist of the novel, and it is especially important to identify some key elements of his social and political context.

Jews have been much discriminated against in the US by the main-stream white Protestant establishment, and prejudice against Jewish scholars in universities and colleges was certainly intense in the 1930s when Trilling was a student and teaching assistant. Hearing that he would be dismissed from Columbia in 1936, a decision that was almost immediately reversed, Trilling recorded in his journal that: 'The reason for dismissal is that as a Jew, a Marxist, a Freudian I am uneasy. This hampers my work and makes me unhappy' (Zinn 1984: 498).

Trilling was ambivalent about his Jewishness. In 1928 he wrote that 'being a Jew is like walking in the wind or swimming: you are touched at all points and conscious everywhere' (Zinn 1984: 496). Yet he observed in 1944 that 'I do not think of myself as a "Jewish" writer' (Simpson 1987: 409). Even at the height of his success, however, he liked to see himself as an outsider figure. This explains, in part, his initial fascination with Marx and his lifelong interest in Freud; for both writers, in complex ways, regarded life as a perpetual struggle against the odds. For Trilling, Marx and Freud unsettled conventional senses of reality by arguing that the authentic self is oppressed, or under siege, from society and culture; and this is very much the theme of *The Opposing Self* (1955b) and *Beyond Culture* (1965). What Trilling endorsed in Freud was less the psychoanalytical side of his project, more his overall focus on 'the complexity, secrecy, and *duplicity* that Freud ascribes to the human mind' (Trilling 1970: 27). The culmin-ation of Trilling's thinking in this area is *Sincerity and Authenticity* (1972), where he argues that 'sincerity' is a self-serving performance in a culture that has to be resisted if any kind of authenticity is to prevail. But even that 'authenticity' comes under suspicion there.

Trilling is often associated with a group of second- and third-generation Jewish immigrants that came to be known as the 'New York Intellectuals'. They first came together (as a loose, informal coalition) in the 1930s, largely through each writer's connections with the journal *Partisan Review*. The *Partisan Review*, which devoted itself to political articles as well as literary criticism, began life uneasily com-mitted to Marxism. The exiled Soviet politician Leon Trotsky was one of its early contributors. Like Trilling himself, however, and the New York Intellectuals in general, it became disaffected with communism as a viable model for revolutionary change in America, not least after news began to emerge in the mid-1930s of Stalin's purges in Soviet Russia. While brutally forcing through his policy of 'collectivization', the state expropriation and control of agriculture, Stalin dealt ruthlessly with his political enemies and those he saw as sympathizing with Trotsky. Trotsky was eventually tracked down in Mexico City by Stalin's agents and murdered in 1940. Countless people, including many army commanders whom Stalin regarded as opponents of communism, were incarcerated and executed. The majority of American Marxist 'fellow-travellers' (communist sympathizers such as Trilling, who held back from actually joining the party), shocked and outraged by what they saw as Stalin's violation of Marxist idealism, deserted communism and attempted to preserve elements of their left-wing sympathies in forms of reconditioned liberalism. This is the specific context of Trilling's novel, *The Middle of the Journey* (1947), which dramatizes the predicament of American supporters of communism in the 1930s. Three years later, in his *The Liberal Imagination*, Trilling went on to attack liberal (by which he meant Marxist) thinkers and critics for their inflexible views, advocating instead a responsible politics that could balance progressive and conservative tendencies.

Nineteen-fifties America, when Dwight David Eisenhower (1890–1969) was elected (1952) and re-elected (1956) president, is often perceived as an era of burgeoning mass-consumption, cultural vulgarity, and reactionary conservatism in America following the communist witch-hunts of Senator Joseph McCarthy (1909–57) in the late 1940s

LIBERALISM

The associations of 'liberalism' in English (and in Britain) are with vague notions of freedom. As it comes down through the English philosopher John Stuart Mill (1806–73) and others, liberal thinking involves the idea that individuals are free as long as that freedom is limited by the needs of other individuals and of the community as a whole. In America today (as it certainly was for Trilling), 'liberalism' is a code-word for radical, progressive, political policies that verge on socialism or even communism. Its use in America is often pejorative. In a definition local to the 1930s and 1940s, Trilling suggested that liberalism involved a 'mild suspiciousness of the profit motive, a belief in progress, science, social legislation, planning, and international cooperation, perhaps especially where Russia is in question' (1950: 93).

and early 1950s. Critics such as Joseph Frank (1956) and Norman Podhoretz (1979) – whom Trilling championed, rather unrewardingly, as a young scholar – suggest that Trilling moved from Marxism in the 1930s, through a sceptical liberalism in the 1940s, to a neoconservative position in the 1950s to which he clung for the rest of his life. This is a political trajectory that reached into the student uprisings, civil rights riots, and anti-Vietnam War demonstrations of the 1960s, a decade which saw the so-called 'counter-cultural' movement, or youth-rebellion, against the conformist 1950s. A basic sense of this political framework is necessary both for an understanding of Trilling's and Booth's approaches to the novel and for a grasp of why they were attracted to the work of Henry James.

Henry James had little interest in or connection with the world of formal education, but for Trilling and Booth, the university was the main institutional context for their writing. Many New York Intellectuals believed, however, that university affiliations compromised their independence as critical outsiders. Trilling was acutely aware of this problem, especially as he persistently sought to communicate with the broadly literate reader in a plain, straightforward kind of prose rather than merely to address an academic audience. In the late 1960s, Trilling wrote that he regarded 'with misgivings the growing affinity between the university and the arts' (1968: 407). Trilling was often, in fact, more a 'public intellectual' (as they are called in America) than a university professor. He undertook editorial work for book societies in the 1950s; and he wrote accessible introductions to a wide range of literary classics. A number of these are collected in *A Gathering of Fugitives* (1956). The professionalization of literary criticism and its expansion in the realms of higher education distinguish the eras of Trilling and Booth from that of James. James, Trilling, and Booth span the movement from a turn-of-the-nineteenth-century literary criticism organized around 'men of letters' and independent scholars to a profession anchored in university teaching and research. Trilling attempted to keep a foot in both camps.

The English departments in which Trilling studied and later taught developed in a period when the 'New Criticism' mentioned at the outset of this chapter held sway. In keeping with the fashion of the time, Trilling (as much a social as a literary critic) was often attacked for concentrating too much on the historical and contemporary contexts of the literature he was considering, at the expense of textual analysis or close reading. This emphasis in Trilling's work can be traced in part to his earlier enthusiasm for Marxism and to his continuing belief in the social and moral relevance of fiction. A belief in the singular importance of this relevance, however differently they might have defined it, is one of the most significant connections between James, Trilling, and Booth.

WAYNE C. BOOTH (1921–2005)

Wayne C. Booth was born at American Fork, Utah, in 1921, and brought up as a Mormon by his parents. Throughout his life, Booth listed himself as 'L.D.S.', signalling his membership of the Church of Jesus Christ of Latter-Day Saints. This was despite long spells of religious scepticism and inactivity. Booth undertook missionary work in his youth for the Mormon Church, and a number of critics, including James Phelan (1988), argue that the zeal of this early experience seems to have carried over into his professional life. He was renowned for being an intense advocate of the moral and social value of studying literature. He had an outstanding reputation as an inspiring teacher, continuing to teach freshmen (first-year students) with alacrity well beyond his formal retirement.

MORMONS

Mormons are members of the Church of Jesus Christ of Latter-Day Saints. The sect was founded in New York by Joseph Smith (1805–44) in 1830. Smith claimed to have discovered, after a divine revelation, the *Book of Mormon* (equally as sacred as the Bible, for Mormons), which tells the story of a group of Hebrews who migrated to America around 600 BC. The sect was notorious for sanctioning polygamy, a practice that was abandoned in 1890. Brigham Young (1801–77) succeeded Smith as leader, and he moved the Mormon headquarters to Salt Lake City, Utah, in 1847. As adventists, or millenarianists, Mormons believe that Jesus Christ will reign in the world for a thousand years after his second coming. There are no professional clergy, and members contribute a proportion of their income (known as 'tithes') to the Church.

Booth graduated in English, having switched from Chemistry, at Brigham Young University (a Mormon institution) in Provo, Utah, in 1944. He served as an infantryman in the United States army between 1944 and 1946 before completing both his MA (1947) and his PhD (1950) at the University of Chicago. After a period of ten years or so of teaching in small colleges, Booth was appointed George M. Pullman Professor of English at the University of Chicago in 1962. *The Rhetoric of Fiction* (1961), his most significant and influential contribution to critical thinking, and a major focus of this book, had been published a year earlier to widespread critical acclaim. It was awarded two prestigious prizes: the Phi Beta Kappa's Christian Gauss Award (1962), and the David H. Russell Award of the National Council of Teachers (1966). In 1970, the University of Chicago bestowed on Booth the title of Distinguished Service Professor. Wayne C. Booth played a full part in the American professional arena, acting as president of the Modern Language Association in 1982. He was also instrumental in establishing in the 1970s the quarterly academic journal, *Critical Inquiry*, which was soon at the forefront of debates about literary theory and criticism.

Like Trilling, Booth had to deal with the student protests of the late 1960s: he was Dean of the College (where the undergraduate teaching takes place in Chicago) from 1964 until 1969, one of the most turbulent periods in the history of American universities. Booth believed that failures of communication at all levels were partly responsible for the problems. As a result, he wrote *Now Don't Try to Reason with Me: Essays and Ironies for a Credulous Age* (1970) and *Modern Dogma and the Rhetoric of Assent* (1974a), arguing that understanding texts, or people, on their own terms in the first instance is the only respectable intellectual position to adopt. This is also very much the informing principle of both *A Rhetoric of Irony* (1974b) and *The Company We Keep: An Ethics of Fiction* (1988a). Fundamental to all these books, and also to *The Rhetoric of Fiction*, is the assumption that the moral health of a reader depends on his or her ability to interact with the author in the meeting place of the text under consideration. The basis of this meeting, Booth holds, should be an acknowledgement of the importance of rhetoric to literature and literary communication. Booth's graduate work at Chicago took place mostly under the supervision of R. S. Crane (1886–1967), one of the foremost members of the Chicago School of criticism. Like the New Critics, the Chicago School

RHETORIC

Rhetoric can be defined as 'the art of using language so as to persuade or influence others' (*Oxford English Dictionary*, 2nd edn). For Aristotle (384–322 BC), the Greek philosopher, every element of a text is part of an overall system of communication designed to persuade the reader into adopting a certain position, or to think and behave in certain ways. The emphasis is on the literary text as a form of communication in which – so Booth would argue, at least – both author and reader have to take a responsible part. The common view of rhetoric is negative: it is regarded as a form of deception. This is a distortion of its original sense. In the last book he published before his death, Booth coined the word 'rhetrickery' for what he calls 'cheating rhetoric' (2004: 41, 44).

emphasized the need to focus on the text, and to move away from context (history and biography, for example). But whereas the concentration in New Criticism was on language, and hence mostly on poetry, critics such as Crane were equally, if not more, interested in the text as a system of communication in which plot, characterization, and overall structure played a part. Members of the Chicago School were often referred to as Neo-Aristotelians because, under the influence of Aristotle, they saw every element of the text, and the text as a whole, as mimetic, as an enactment of the experience or reality being represented.

Above all, Crane and his fellow critics argued that there can be no single way of approaching a literary text: this is known as a 'pluralist' approach. On what the critic chooses to focus will shape the questions he or she asks and the language and concepts used. There should be no dogmatism about such issues. In *The Rhetoric of Fiction*, as we shall see, Booth puzzled over the boundary between text and world insisted on by both the New Critics and the Chicago School, and his debt to critical pluralism is evident most strongly in *Critical Understanding: The Powers and Limits of Pluralism* (1979). All of these issues relate to that concept of rhetoric, and to the way in which texts are construed as systematic forms of persuasion. The vital importance of this concept to Booth is clear from the appearance in 2004, when he was eighty-three, of *The Rhetoric of Rhetoric: The Quest for Effective Communication*.

CHICAGO SCHOOL: PRINCIPAL IDEAS

Like the New Critics, critics in the Chicago School focused on the text; but unlike the New Critics, they saw language as only one of its elements. Their emphasis was on the whole structure, not just as a form of communication, but as a system of persuasion that enacted, or was mimetic of the experience it represented. Each text can (and needs) to be approached in a number of different ways by the reader and critic.

It is rhetoric, then, that will underpin much of our discussion of Booth's work and its relation to that of James and Trilling.

Wayne C. Booth died on 10 October 2005, within a week of my finishing this book. But as his work everywhere testifies, at least he managed to live first.

It is worth reminding ourselves, having considered the lives of these theorists alongside one another, that each existed within a powerful religious context: James contended with the legacy of Puritanism, Trilling was a Jew, however uneasily, and Booth was an active Mormon in his youth. The religious dimensions in the work of all three help to explain the moral intensity of their approaches to fiction and the novel. As Trilling himself expressed it in *The Liberal Imagination*:

> Loosely put, the idea is that religion in its decline leaves a detritus of pieties, of strong assumptions, which afford a particularly fortunate condition for certain kinds of literature; these pieties carry a strong charge of intellect, or perhaps it would be more accurate to say that they tend to stimulate the mind in a powerful way.

(1950: 282)

These religious remains, or 'detritus of pieties', can also be seen, in part, as what compel the interest of these three writers in questions of reading, close reading, and interpretation: going beyond the literal, or surface, meaning of the text is a form of reading habitually applied to sacred writings such as the Christian Bible, the Jewish Talmud, and the Book of Mormon. This, in Trilling's case, also takes us back to Freud and his ideas about dreams. Trilling notes with approval Freud's belief that 'the "manifest content" of a literary work, like that of a patient's dream . . . is qualified, sometimes contradicted, always enriched, by the "latent content" that can be discovered lying beneath it' (1970: 27).

THIS BOOK

The starting-point of this book is the idea that Henry James, Lionel Trilling, and Wayne C. Booth shared an interest in the relation, seen largely in terms of communication, between fiction and the world, especially in the moral and artistic values of the novel and its effects on senses of the self.

If the novel is a communication process consisting in part of a real author, text, and reader, then there is also the question, for Booth, of what version of the author (the 'implied author') is projected in the text, or what composite sense ('career author') we develop as we read two or more novels by the same writer, how the story is told (what kind of narrator or narrative method is used), any characters who may 'listen' to or 'read' the story in the text (the 'narratees'), and the type of reader constructed or implied in the text, as distinct from any actual reader. Framing all this are the societies inhabited by author and reader. After *The Rhetoric of Fiction*, Booth calls the real author and the real reader the 'flesh-and-blood author' and the 'flesh-and-blood reader' (1988a: 134–5) in order to detach them even more emphatically from their 'career' and 'implied' versions. In *The Rhetoric of Fiction* and, later, in *The Company We Keep: An Ethics of Fiction*, Booth makes explicit many of the elements involved in the production and reception of fiction implicit in the criticism of James and Trilling. We can represent this communication process using the model shown below (p. 16), which has been adapted from Booth.

The elements in bold italics nominally lie within the boundaries of the text; but these are permeable boundaries as we shall see. The double-headed arrows indicate that none of these relations is one-way. The 'author's character' (or 'image') is the 'image' of the author 'created and played with by author' (often in autobiography and interviews) and his or her 'public' (Booth 1979: 271). This image is the product, then, not just of literary criticism, but of advertising and the PR machine. It is quite independent of, and sometimes at odds with, the texts themselves. The 'career author' is in square brackets here to represent the fact that he or she is neither in any one text, nor outside,

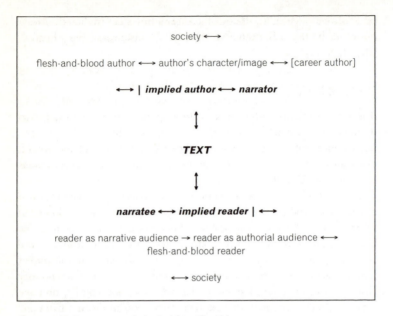

society ←→

flesh-and-blood author ←→ author's character/image ←→ [career author]

←→ | *implied author* ←→ *narrator*

↕

TEXT

↕

narratee ←→ *implied reader* | ←→

reader as narrative audience → reader as authorial audience ←→
flesh-and-blood reader

←→ society

Communication process (adapted from Booth)

but an abstraction from two or more texts. The way readers build up a composite sense of this career author by reading more than one of his or her novels is considered in Chapter 5. The reader as part of a 'narrative' and 'authorial' audience will also be discussed more fully in that chapter. The Key Ideas section of this book is organized around this model, with each chapter focusing on certain elements or relations within the communicative process between text and the world. The elements of this process are neither equally important, nor necessarily the same, for all three critics. For this reason, the degree to which each writer moves in and out of focus depends on the topics under scrutiny and will vary from chapter to chapter.

As we have seen from our discussion of the lives and contexts of these writers, they all wrote extensively. This book, however, is anchored in Henry James's 'The Art of Fiction' (1884) and his prefaces to the New York Edition of his novels and tales (1907–9), in Lionel Trilling's *The Liberal Imagination* (1950), *The Opposing Self* (1955b), *Beyond Culture* (1965), and *Sincerity and Authenticity* (1972), and Wayne C. Booth's *The Rhetoric of Fiction* (1961) and *The Company We Keep*

(1988a). It is a guide to the ideas of these three theorists, and to these (their major) texts. But other works will be considered, or signposted, where appropriate.

Chapter 1, 'Three perspectives on the novel' surveys the ways in which James, Trilling, and Booth define the novel (and, more broadly, fiction in general) and its purpose, and on how all three attempt to rescue the form from its compromising popularity by elevating it to the level of an art.

Among the questions to be considered in Chapter 2, 'Realism and representation', are: What role can the writer have if the main purpose of a novel is faithfully to depict experience? Can there be any agreement about what 'faithful depiction' amounts to? What happens if a novelist abandons realism? Is it possible to strike a balance between being excessively concerned with formal, structural properties, in fiction and the commitment to some form of representation?

Ideas about 'Authors, narrators, and narration' figure in Chapter 3 where the views of James, Trilling, and Booth on the troublesome boundary between life (including the lives of authors) and fiction are explored. How far, if at all, should authors obtrude in their fiction? Is their detachment necessarily healthy for the reader? Should fiction, or critical approaches to it, be biographical? Does Booth's emphasis on rhetoric, on the novel as a form of persuasion, necessarily involve the rejection of experimental novels where the meaning is deliberately obscure or unavailable?

At the core of Chapter 4, 'Points of view and centres of consciousness', is that all-important narrative device for James of point of view. Trilling's formal interests are much thinner than those of James and Booth, so the main focus here is on them. Does an emphasis on 'consciousness' result in exaggerating the importance of individual thought at the expense of social and political problems at large? Does it lead to elitist novels that cannot, and will not, address these problems? Does complication become more important than communication? Did James advocate restricting the point of view from which the story is told to one character? Are there any correspondences here with the early twentieth-century fashion for relativity and multiple perspectives? Are there connections between these ideas and Trilling's attempts to renovate notions of 'liberalism' in the late 1940s and early 1950s? Is Booth right to be concerned about the moral consequences of multiplied perspectives and narrative ambiguities, or confusions?

Chapter 5 concentrates on 'Readers, reading, and interpretation'. It continues, in part, to pursue the issue of communication raised in this section on p. 16. Should the writer aim for a wide readership if the responsibilities of the novel are seen in social and political terms? What conflicts might there be here between more artistic, aesthetic, approaches to writing fiction? Can interpretation be controlled? Should it be controlled? Is this what Booth means, for example, by 'understanding?' What responsibilities, if any, does the reader have when it comes to interpretation and criticism?

'Moral intelligence', the sixth chapter, consolidates much of the previous discussion by exploring (and encouraging debate about) how James, Trilling, and Booth discuss the moral and ethical dimensions of the writing and reading of fiction. If rule-bound, didactic novels are condemned as inartistic, are the alternatives moral relativism and anarchy? James and Trilling seem to argue that the best guarantee of responsible behaviour lies in the cultivation of individual intelligence, of flexible thinking, whereas Booth is often more interested in advocating a much less flimsy framework of clear moral principles in which communication and consensus are among the controlling elements. Is a resolution of these conflicts between Booth on the one hand, and James and Trilling on the other, desirable, or even possible?

The penultimate section, 'After James, Trilling, and Booth', will look at where these critics have left us, and at the current state of the debates in which they are involved. The book concludes with a guide to 'Further reading' on these three theorists.

KEY IDEAS

THREE PERSPECTIVES
ON THE NOVEL

This chapter has at its centre the various ways in which James, Trilling, and Booth defined the novel and its purpose. It begins by focusing on Henry James's 'The Art of Fiction' (1884), an essay that set the agenda for contemporary debates and later discussions. After considering James's approach to fiction and the novel in this influential essay, it will be much easier to see why Lionel Trilling recruits it as his main ally in the cultural and political battles of the 1940s and beyond. It will also become clear, as we turn to Wayne C. Booth and *The Rhetoric of Fiction*, why Booth had mixed feelings about James's theories of the novel. Many of the issues raised in this chapter will be considered in more detail in the rest of the book.

HENRY JAMES AND 'THE ART OF FICTION'

As we saw in the introductory section of the book ('Why James, Trilling, and Booth?'), the novel has struggled to be taken seriously as an art form. The very title of James's essay begins his campaign on its behalf: 'art' and 'fiction', often seen at odds with each other, are placed side by side here. Prose fiction includes short stories, novellas (longer short stories), and the novel. James regarded the novel as supreme in its importance, not least because of the possibilities it provided for larger-scale plot development and characterization. In this

THE NOVEL

'Novel' derives from the Italian word *novella*, which means 'tale', or 'piece of news'. As they came into prominence in the early eighteenth century, novels were mainly concerned with the representation of everyday events, or (generally) the fairly recent past, rather than with the universal truth to which poets and playwrights often seemed to aspire. The *OED* (*Oxford English Dictionary*) defines the novel as 'a fictitious prose narrative or tale of considerable length . . . in which characters and actions representative of the real life of past or present times are portrayed in a plot of more or less complexity'.

essay, as Mark Spilka has argued, James began 'an adventure of immense importance to the novel's history' (1977: 208).

James begins by referring to 'the mystery of story-telling' (1884: 44), and it is worth reminding ourselves that the word 'mystery' originally referred to the secrets of a particular trade, or craft, and that 'art' was generally applied in mediaeval times and beyond to practical skills. James's perspective in this essay is very much that of the producer, of the novelist, and he wants to retrieve this older, practical sense of 'art', together with the meaning that developed in the Romantic period (in literature, from around the 1780s through to the 1830s). In that period, artists were regarded as creative geniuses involved in the production of beautiful artefacts. What defined art, increasingly in the nineteenth century, was its detachment from the world, or its apparent lack of a specifiable purpose. The best fiction, for James, is an art because it involves both the kind of proficiency in a craft that comes with a long apprenticeship and the individual creative genius celebrated by Romantic writers such as the English poets William Wordsworth (1770–1850) and John Keats (1795–1821). By combining these meanings of 'art', James attempts to fend off those who attack the novel for having 'no great character' and for being a 'commodity so quickly and easily produced' (1884: 49).

At the core of James's definition of the novel is what he sees as its responsibility to represent life. He states that this is 'the only reason for the existence of a novel' (1884: 46). But it soon emerges that

James is committed to a complex and shifting sense of what this responsibility amounts to. Part of the reason for these complications is James's belief that 'a novel ought to be artistic' (1884: 47) as well as a representation of life. In an era of burgeoning popular photography, James wants to put as much distance as possible between the novel and crude realism. He argues that '[a] novel is in its broadest definition a personal, a direct impression of life' (1884: 50). Crucially important here is the imaginative power of the writer; and this is what distinguishes the good novel from the bad, or popular, novel. To write artistic novels, rather than novels merely, the author must have '[t]he power to guess the unseen from the seen, to trace the implication of things, to judge the whole piece by the pattern' (1884: 53).

A novel should seek not only to represent life, then, but to refract that representation through faculties of the imagination sharpened by sensitive and responsive observations in the world of experience. To say that novels represent experience realistically and leave it at that is to fail to acknowledge 'that experience is never limited', and that 'it is never complete' (1884: 52). It is also to overlook that 'the measure of reality is very difficult to fix' (1884: 51). James is less interested in 'reality', much more in the 'air of reality' (1884: 53). The central appeal of the novel is in its ability to represent life so interestingly that it actually 'competes' with it (1884: 53). Indeed, James was to go much further than this in a letter to the English novelist H. G. Wells (1866–1946), arguing there that 'it is art that *makes* life' (1915: 770). At the very least – because of its scope, flexibility of form, and openness towards experimentation – the novel can have the 'large, free character of an immense and exquisite correspondence with life' (1884: 61).

If the novel is a representation of life, its own vitality comes in part from the fusion of that representation with the writer's own impressions. James's insistence on the need for novels to be vital, on the analogy between the novel as a form and life, has a significant bearing on his theories of fiction and definition of the novel:

I cannot imagine composition existing in a series of blocks ... A novel is a living thing, all one and continuous, like any other organism, and in proportion as it lives will it be found, I think, that in each of the parts there is something of each of the other parts.

(1884: 54)

We shall return to this aspect of James's definition of the novel later in the book. What matters here is the emphasis on the artificial nature of any boundaries between character and story, or plot, dialogue, description, and narration. James saw novels, in keeping with his description of them as 'the most human form of art' (1880: 868), as 'organic' in form. This fear of writing in 'blocks' is partly what propels James into condemning novels where the author's voice, or that of his narrator, is obtrusive. If we return to the model of narrative as communication introduced on p. 16, it becomes clear that James is intent on constructing novels as highly organized entities in which the boundaries (marked in the model by vertical lines) between the text and life, or the worlds of the author and reader, are firm. James was unhappy with facile connections between text and author, and anxious about destructive interferences from the reader at large.

Further at issue are what James regarded as fruitless distinctions, then common, between 'the novel of character and the novel of incident' (1884: 54). James was often criticized for focusing too much on psychological analysis at the expense of telling a good story, for elaborating on character rather than concentrating on the plot; and his defence is that the boundaries between these are useless. Such separations result in a dead rather than a living work of art. He regarded characters as analogous to the seeds of a plant: the novel should develop outwardly from the nature of those characters, the plot resulting from their characteristics and not the other way round.

James extends his application of the biological metaphor of an organism when identifying the 'search for form' (1884: 48) as a central feature of the art of fiction. The search, among other things, is for the most effective way of structuring and narrating the story as a whole; and it can only be found from within the subject itself, not by imposing existing patterns or applying sterile rules. In his preface to *The Spoils of Poynton*, James calls this 'the logic of the particular case' (1907–9: 1139). This view leads not just to a rejection of any externally imposed purpose on the novel, in keeping with the idea of organic form, but to the repudiation of any kind of 'conscious moral purpose' (1884: 62). The alternative is to confine the subject to 'conventional, traditional moulds', thereby reducing it to 'an eternal repetition of a few familiar *clichés*' (1884: 58). It is a 'mistake' to 'say so definitely beforehand what sort of an affair the good novel will be'; the 'only obligation

ORGANIC FORM

At the end of the eighteenth century, it became common for German philosophers such as Immanuel Kant (1724–1804) and August Wilhelm Schlegel (1767–1845) to insist on the distinction between 'mechanical' and 'organic' form. This distinction had a strong influence on the English poet Samuel Taylor Coleridge (1772–1834) and found its way into American thinking largely through the writings of the New England essayist and poet Ralph Waldo Emerson (1803–82). Where the form is mechanical, the parts of any object (such as a watch) are brought together from the outside by some external agent and the object is simply the sum of its parts. As Coleridge expressed it: 'The form is mechanic, when on any given material we impress a pre-determined form, not necessarily arising out of the properties of the material ... The organic form, on the other hand is innate; it shapes, as it develops, itself from within' (Coleridge 1811–18: 229). If the form is organic (as in a tree), the object (or organism) develops from some central point in the subject itself and is not shaped by outside considerations; and, as James says in 'The Art of Fiction', in 'each of the parts there is something of each of the other parts' (1884: 54). An organism, unlike a mechanism, is a whole which is greater than the sum of its parts. For James, this became the most important model for the structure of the novel. It is one of the aspects of his thinking on which the New Critics seized.

to which in advance we may hold a novel . . . is that it be interesting' (1884: 49).

'The Art of Fiction' is in large measure a rebuttal of the English novelist and critic Walter Besant's *The Art of Fiction* (1884), from where James initially took his title, and its insistence on the novel as an 'Art' which is 'governed and directed by general laws' (Besant 1884: 3). The most important of these laws was that there should be a 'conscious moral purpose' (Besant 1884: 24). Against this, James asserts that '[t]here are bad novels and good novels', but 'that is the only distinction in which I see any meaning' (James 1884: 55). The implications of what he goes on to say for the relation between the novel and morality are at the centre of Chapter 6:

> There is one point at which the moral sense and the artistic sense lie very near together; that is in the light of the very obvious truth that the deepest quality of a work of art will always be the quality of the mind of the producer ... No good novel will ever proceed from a superficial mind.
>
> (1884: viii)

The author should be granted his 'subject' (1884: 56), the form of which 'is to be appreciated after the fact' (1884: 50). If the reader dislikes the subject, then the novel can be abandoned. The measure of a novel's success is that of how the subject is treated; whether it develops organically, that is, like a seed into a plant, from the centre of its chosen subject. '[W]e can estimate quality', James believed, only by applying the 'test of execution' (1884: 50), by judging what an author has done with his or her subject. James criticized George Eliot's *Middlemarch* (1871–2), for example, for being a 'treasure-house of details', but an 'indifferent whole' (Rawlings 2002: 2: 301). He saw the character of Dorothea as central to the novel and felt that excursions into other characters and stories were a distraction. For James, George Eliot's novel not only dealt with its subject in too scattered and distracting a way, it was ultimately irresponsive and irresponsible to what should have been its subject, Dorothea, thereby failing the 'test of execution'.

LIONEL TRILLING AND *THE LIBERAL IMAGINATION*

In the feverish political climate of the 1930s and 1940s outlined in the introductory section, American critics with left-wing sympathies turned James's disavowal of any direct purpose for the novel against him. They approved of writers such as Theodore Dreiser (1871–1945) and John Steinbeck (1902–68) who specialized in documenting the oppressive conditions of many American workers and the general plight of the under-classes. For Trilling, in a phrase to which we shall return, Dreiser and James were 'at the dark and bloody crossroads where literature and politics meet' (Trilling 1950: 10). Far from aligning himself, however, with what the nineteenth-century English critic Walter Pater (1893–94) had called 'the love of art for its own sake' (1893: 190), Trilling positions himself and Henry James as being political in the broader senses clarified and explored in *The Liberal Imagination*.

The Liberal Imagination is organized as a series of essays rather than as the unified study of a particular author or narrowly defined topic. Given that this chapter is concerned in a preliminary way with perspectives on the novel, the main focus here will be on the essays devoted to it: 'Reality in America', 'The Princess Casamassima' (one of Henry James's novels), and arguably two of the most important and challenging chapters in the book: 'Manners, Morals, and the Novel' and 'Art and Fortune'. Trilling was attracted to the essay form partly because of the variety of topics and approaches it allowed; but he was also committed to the more casual, less sternly systematic, tone and conversational style he was able to develop in shorter pieces. As Roger Sale has characterized it: 'The voice of The Liberal Imagination . . . speaks from a lectern: here is a subject, a problem, a matter for an hour's serious thought, let us see what we can say about it' (1973: 328).

But Sale's qualified approval of this method is far from universally shared: Denis Donoghue, for example, disparaged Trilling by observing that he was 'likely to remain' merely 'the Intelligent Man's Guide to Literature' (Donoghue 1955: 222). For Robert Mazzocco, 'the usual impression' of Trilling's prose 'is that of trudging uphill, scanning hazy vistas martyred with abstractions' (Mazzocco 1965: 260). This assessment, however, tells us as much about the fracture opening up between scientific and humane approaches to literature in the 1960s as it does about the effectiveness of Trilling's style. All Trilling's publications after The Liberal Imagination consist of essay or lecture collections.

Despite the apparently miscellaneous nature of The Liberal Imagination, its constituent parts are held together by the broad political agenda signalled in its title. In the face of what he saw as the dogmatism of socialists and communist sympathizers, Trilling establishes an 'abiding interest' (1950: i) in his introduction, which turns out to be quite closely connected with the various functions he goes on to identify for the novel form itself: 'The job of criticism would seem to be, then, to recall liberalism to its first essential imagination of variousness and possibility, which implies the awareness of complexity and difficulty' (1950: vi).

The problem with Marxist theories, which Trilling expresses in a way that recalls James's insistence on organic form, is in their 'mechanical' (1950: v) view of the world. In line with Henry James's 'The Art of Fiction', Trilling argues that literature, and especially the novel, 'is the human activity that takes the fullest and most precise account of variousness, possibility, complexity, and difficulty' (1950: vii).

At first sight, though, categories such as 'variousness' and 'difficulty' seem like huge abstractions from the real world; and this is a problem that Trilling tries to tackle in the chapter entitled 'Reality in America'. For Trilling, the left's critical approval of Dreiser's fiction at the expense of Henry James was flawed by a misguided belief in the value of novels that represented the world in straightforward, documentary ways, simplifying both the problem (as a class struggle between factory owners and their employees, for example) and its solution (the need for revolution). Trilling abhorred the movement of some American novelists into this kind of 'social realism' between the First and Second World Wars. The American literary historian V. L. Parrington (1871–1929), whose *Main Currents in American Thought* (1927–30) is a target in 'Reality in America', was an advocate if not of social realism, then of novels that depict social problems with the aim of bringing about reform. Parrington is memorably described by Trilling as having 'a limited sense of what constitutes a difficulty' (1950: 4). It is precisely this limitation that the novel, especially as handled by James, can and should confront. What James's theory and practice as a novelist display is a 'moral mind' with an 'awareness of tragedy, irony, and multitudinous distinctions' (1950: 10). At the heart of the novel is not the 'current', suggesting a simple flow, of Parrington's title, but struggle, debate, and 'contradictions' (1950: 9). Novels written within this paradigm, or to this model, could challenge the valorization of 'dullness and stupidity' all too easily entailed by reductive notions of 'virtuous democracy' (1950: 11). In short, their task is to counter the 'political', or Marxist, 'fear of the intellect' (1950: 11).

In his approach to James's *The Princess Casamassima*, Trilling identifies two aspects of fiction as being of equal importance to the novel: 'illusion', with 'primitive' narratives such as the fairy-tale as a vital part of its syntax, and 'probability', within a framework of 'verisimilitude' or 'truth' (1950: 62, 63). Trilling recognizes that the balance between the two is a shifting one; but he insists that no novelist should adhere slavishly, as critics such as Parrington seemed to advocate, to 'multitudinous records' (1950: 65). James's novel, as many of the best novels are, is 'a brilliantly precise representation of social actuality' (1950: 71); but its power is in the pursuit of the 'analogue of art with

SOCIAL REALISM

'Social realism' has its roots in the early twentieth-century Russian theatre and one of its main theorists was Anatoli Lunacharsky (1875–1933). He believed that classic plays should be reinterpreted from the point of view of contemporary relevance and that new plays should focus on the lives of ordinary people. In Soviet Russia under Stalin, social realism developed into 'socialist realism': the artist was regarded merely as a servant of the state whose task was to support Marxism. American fiction stressing social problems and the hardships of everyday life evolved within a context of 'naturalism', a form of realism that thrived at the turn of the nineteenth century and which emphasized the seamier side of life and the extent to which individuals have little or no freedom of choice in society. In America, Theodore Dreiser, Frank Norris (1870–1902), and Stephen Crane (1871–1900) typify this movement. Dreiser's *Sister Carrie* (1900), Norris's *The Octopus* (1901), and Crane's *Maggie: A Girl of the Streets* (1893) are representative works of fiction in this tradition. After renouncing Marxism, Trilling became radically opposed to what he saw as the anti-individualism of this genre.

power' (1950: 79). Worrying once more about what he sees as the simplifications of Marxism, Trilling argues that the novel should seek out the complications of the 'moral mind' (1950: 10) rather than merely serve the needs of 'our facile sociological minds' (1950: 83). Trilling in this essay at least, like James, is committed to the principles of organic unity: *The Princess Casamassima* is praised for its 'complex totality'. James's novel is also endorsed for its 'incomparable representation of the spiritual circumstances of our civilization' (1950: 88).

Trilling is close to James in that his emphasis is on the novel as a representation of life; its 'art', as for James, is in the interaction between that representation and the writer's impressions, in an imaginative sense of the subject. Trilling's concern, by contrast with James, however, is much more with the 'society' element in our narrative model (p. 16); on the social context, that is, of both author and reader, and on the novel's responsibilities towards the morality, broadly defined, of the community. As the American critic Norman Podhoretz

has it: Trilling 'understood literature as an act of the moral imagination and as an agent of social and political health' (Podhoretz 1968: 79).

Trilling's definition of the novel and its particular significance culminates in *The Liberal Imagination* in two of its major essays: 'Manners,
Morals, and the Novel' and 'Art and Fortune'. The first essay will be
at the centre of Chapter 6, 'Moral intelligence'. But it is important to
note here that in that essay Trilling qualifies his stress on the importance of 'reality' for the novel by turning it into the 'question of reality'
and adding that its focus has actually tended to be on 'the old opposition between reality and appearance, between what really is and what
merely seems' (1950: 195). It is not 'reality' that is essential to the
novel, but the 'question of reality', the 'problem of reality' (1950:
196). This is especially evident in the novel's entanglement with money
and what it symbolizes. Money is 'the great generator of illusion',
closely bound up as it is with 'snobbery'. For Trilling, the 'novel is
born in response to snobbery' (1950: 197). Money, nothing in itself,
is significant only in terms of how it is perceived and appears; and its
appearance, like all appearances, is a false one. Snobbery involves a
misguided deference towards what are regarded as superior and often
steeply hierarchical social structures. The 'characteristic work of the
novel is to record the illusion that snobbery generates and to try to
penetrate to the truth which, as the novel assumes, lies hidden beneath
all false appearances' (1950: 198).

At the centre of such illusions, then, are money and the fantasies
and delusions of power to which it gives rise. It is within this context
that the novel 'is a perpetual quest for reality', the 'field of its research
being always the social world', and 'the material of its analysis
being always manners as the indication of the direction of man's soul'
(1950: 199). For the social realist, the task of the novel is to represent for condemnation an image of society; for Trilling, that image
masks the essential moral complexity with which the novel should
really be engaged.

'Art or Misfortune' considers whether or not the novel is dead as
a form. Trilling argues, recalling once more the concept of organic
form, that 'technique has its autonomy and that it dictates the laws of
its own growth' (1950: 241–2). But relying only on those laws, which
was James's tendency, would result in the exhaustion of the form.
The novel exists in an environment, like any organism, and its existence is conditioned. What conditions the novel is the work for which

it has been contrived. Unlike James, who rejects an externally imposed purpose for the novel, Trilling sees the 'investigation of reality and illusion' (1950: 242), in ways that connect 'Art and Misfortune' with 'Manners, Morals, and the Novel', as its supreme task. Specifically, he again underlines the fact that the relation between reality and illusion can best be considered in conjunction with social class and money. 'Money is both real and not real, like a spook', and what characterizes the novel is its 'interest in illusion and reality as generated by class and money' (1950: 242, 243).

Trilling further suggests that 'the great work' of the novel 'of our time is the restoration and reconstitution of the will' (1950: 250–1) which is dying in our society 'of its own excess' (1950: 250). What matters is the world of 'unfolding possibility', an 'awareness of the will in its beautiful circuit of thought and desire' (1950: 252). The novel is the perfect vehicle for challenging the sterilities of systematic thinking, and for opposing dogmatism and its stifling of spontaneity. The novel is a social affair; but if it is to help in this renovation of the will, it must also concentrate on 'ideas' even though it will be attacked by Marxists for doing so. Trilling's own novel, *The Middle of the Journey*, deals with the plight of intellectuals caught up in competing reactionary and Marxist ideologies; and Trilling firmly believed that that is where novels should be.

The distance between James and Trilling on these issues, in terms of a purpose for the novel beyond the merely aesthetic, is more apparent than real, however. On the one hand, unlike James, Trilling thought that the novel 'achieves its best effects of art often when it

WILL

The will (as in free will) is the power of choice. More broadly, it relates to desires, wishes, and inclinations. For the philosopher Friedrich Nietzsche (1844–1900), it was the basic drive of all human behaviour towards self-mastery which, if frustrated, or inhibited, becomes the will to dominate others. Trilling is not systematically appropriating Nietzsche in *The Liberal Imagination*, but he clearly values the imagination, self-assertion, danger, and originality Nietzsche opposes to the sterile piling up of facts (in *Thus Spoke Zarathustra*, 1888–5, and *Beyond Good and Evil*, 1886).

has no concern with them' (1950: 260), and that 'the novel is . . . the least "artistic" of genres' (1950: 261). Yet on the other, in strains similar to those of 'The Art of Fiction', he believed that it is in the novel that 'thought and desire' can have a 'field of possibility' which, by definition, should not be 'demanded or prescribed or provided for' (1950: 262, 263). James opposes the novel as an organism to Besant's mechanical sense of how it works; and similarly, Trilling counters crude Marxism with what he sees as biological reality. The novel is 'involved with ideas' because 'it deals with man in society' (1950: 265); and ideas are 'living things, inescapably connected with our wills and desires' and 'susceptible of growth and development'. If we think in this way, then the novel as an 'active' form is 'possible' (1950: 284). James and Trilling are at one when it comes to the need for novels to interrogate the 'moral life' (carefully defined). For Trilling, as for James, the greatness of the novel is

> in its unremitting work of involving the reader himself in the moral life, inviting him to put his own motives under examination, suggesting that reality is not as his conventional education has led him to see it. It taught us, as no other genre ever did, the extent of human variety and the value of this variety.
>
> (1950: 209)

For James, too, the supreme value of the novel form is its flexibility and variety: 'the Novel remains still . . . the most independent, most elastic, most prodigious of literary forms' (James 1907–9: 1321). Mark Krupnick pithily expresses the agenda of *The Liberal Imagination* when he proposes that 'Trilling offers the literary imagination as a cure for the simplifications of the liberal imagination' (Krupnick 1986: 63).

WAYNE C. BOOTH AND *THE RHETORIC OF FICTION*

In his 1979 study, *Critical Understanding: The Powers and Limits of Pluralism*, Booth argues that there are five ways of approaching novels, or literary texts. The critic James Phelan summarizes these as follows:

> as an imitation of the world external to it (the mimetic approach), as an event in time (the historical approach), as an autotelic object (the objective), as

an expression – and revelation – of its author's psychology or experience (the
expressive or biographical), as a communication to an audience (rhetorical or
reader-response).

(Phelan 1988: 63)

The next chapter will concentrate on the first, the mimetic. The New
Critics saw the text as autotelic, as a structure of words independent
of its context, but Booth's emphasis is on a textual environment of
communication and reception. In his 'Afterword' to the second edition
of *The Rhetoric of Fiction*, Wayne C. Booth makes it clear that (unlike
Trilling's) his project is trans-historical and non-political: 'studying
the rhetoric of fiction is one thing and studying the political history
of novels . . . is another' (Booth 1983a: 413). Whether such a project
is possible, productive, or welcome is another matter.

Booth's entire approach to the novel is determined by his convic-
tion that '[t]he novel comes into existence as something communicable' (1961: 397). It is, or rather should be, an 'essentially public'
form (1961: 395). Throughout *The Rhetoric of Fiction* and *The Company
We Keep*, the focus is on fiction 'viewed as the art of communicating
with readers' (1961: xiii). In terms of our communication model of
narrative (p. 16), itself mainly derived from Booth, it is not just that
the key elements in *The Rhetoric of Fiction* are the author, text, and
reader; the concentration is on how these interact (or are thought of
as interacting) in the process of writing and reading a novel. As Booth
acknowledges, 'James began at a different place entirely, with the
effort to portray a convincing mind at work on reality' (1961: 43).
It is worth issuing a health warning at this point: an enormous amount
of fiction is discussed or referred to by Booth, and there can be no
expectation that his readers (or the readers of this book) can have read
and assimilated all this material. Everything is to be gained, however,
by reading more of the novels that surface in his argument.

Booth sees the author's central task as that of transmitting to the
reader a clear sense of a fictional world and its moral problems. Crucial
to this act of communication is the extent to which the forms of
rhetoric it adopts are effective to its purpose. There is no time in *The
Rhetoric of Fiction* for what Booth projects as solitary, self-regarding,
experimental novels that privilege the complex and meandering
visions of idiosyncratic writers. Retreating to a 'private world of
values' may be one response to a 'fragmented society', but the purpose

IMPERSONALITY AND NARRATIVE

The French novelist Gustave Flaubert (1821–80) is identified by Booth as an initiator of the fashion in the later nineteenth century for less intrusive narrators in fiction, and for novels (to use Booth's terms) that 'show' rather than 'tell' (Booth 1961: 3–20); a distinction Booth rejects. This is sometimes referred to as a 'dramatic' method because the emphasis is often on scene (or dialogue) and panoramic summary, or pictorial presentation, rather than on narrative commentary and explanation. This fashion hardened into dogma after Percy Lubbock's *The Craft of Fiction* (1921), a book that teased out of Henry James's prefaces (mistakenly, as we shall see in Chapter 4) a systematic theory of impersonal narration.

of the novel in such a world should be to 'mold a new consensus' (1961: 393). If Trilling's antagonists in *The Liberal Imagination* are novels committed to social realism and political propaganda, Booth's are works of fiction that offer peculiar and confused social and moral perspectives, or novels that distinguish themselves as 'pure' because they strive for a seemingly impersonal style with no detectable perspective at all. The reader is offered little guidance in a world of moral complexity often intensified, for the sake of entertainment and technical display, by the multiplication of unresolvable ambiguities and interminable symbolism.

Booth has in mind novels such as the Austrian Franz Kafka's (1883–1924) *The Castle* (1937) where '[n]o one tells us . . . what K's goal is, or whether it is attainable, or whether it is a worthwhile goal in the first place' (Booth 1961: 287). He saw 'deliberate confusion' (1961: 285) as a disease of the modern novel, and the Irish writer James Joyce (1882–1941) as one of its first proponents. Booth also criticizes James's *The Turn of the Screw* (1898) for its muddled and muddling narrative and absence of any clear moral position. It will become clear as the book proceeds, however, that Booth's enduring legacy is less his rather inflexible views on morality, and much more the vocabulary and concepts he developed in order to explore what he sees as the gains and losses of impersonal narration.

For Booth, the main tool for the writer and critic of the novel is rhetoric, the means by which a particular author's fictional world and its moral norms are communicated to the reader. Booth sets out to consider 'whether rhetoric is compatible with art' (1961: xiv) and ends up concluding that every move a writer makes is rhetorical: fiction is rhetoric. Booth demonstrates that despite the claims of the purists, each element of a novel (including dialogue, setting, symbolism, and so on) is part of its system of persuasion. As we have seen, there are two extremes in the spectrum of rhetoric available to the novelist: the use of garrulous narrators who obstruct at every opportunity the reader's own access to the fictional world; and the elimination of such narrators to the point where the reader is left drifting. An example of the former would be the narrator in Henry Fielding's (1707–54) novel, *Tom Jones* (1749), and the French writer Alain Robbe-Grillet's (1922–) *Jealousy* (1957) is offered by Booth as an example of the latter (1961: 62). Although Booth feels able (grudgingly) to 'endure' its 'unmediated, mindless sensation or emotion' because it is 'less than 35,000 words long' (1961: 63), he was generally repelled by the development in the 1950s of the *nouveau roman* in France. By the mid-twentieth century, in the culmination of that process which started with Flaubert and others in the mid-nineteenth century, only novels in the 'pure' category were regarded by many critics and readers as 'realistic', or convincing. What *The Rhetoric of Fiction* sets out to deny is the validity of any distinction between 'pure' and 'impure' fiction.

For Booth, ultimately, distinctions between 'pure form', 'moral content', and the 'rhetorical means of realizing for the reader the union of form and matter' are arbitrary because novels are 'human actions', and 'moral judgments . . . are implicit whenever human beings act' (1961: 397). It is almost impossible to detach any move Booth makes on the novel from his overriding moral concerns; but we shall not really be occupied with these in this section as they figure prominently in Chapter 6. It is worth noting here, however, that the inseparability

NOUVEAU ROMAN

Novelists in this tradition include Alain Robbe-Grillet (1922–), Michel Butor (1926–), Marguerite Duras (1914–96), and Claude Mauriac (1914–96). Rejecting explicit moral, social, or psychological commentary, they focus instead on the detailed description of mental states.

of form and content, and form and morality, is specified by Booth as inherent to novels that communicate successfully. This inseparability is formulated in organic terms ('the unions of form and matter') shared by Trilling and that reach back to James's 'The Art of Fiction'.

For those who abhor 'the modern love of generalization' (1961: 29), and Booth is at one with James and Trilling here, the novel is the most appropriate form of art. Booth endorses James's insistence on the absurdity of applying general laws to the writing of fiction. Novelists are not, or should not be, bound by one method. They can create 'peculiar literary kinds', each of which, like James's 'subjects' in 'The Art of Fiction', entails its own appropriate technique (Booth 1961: 35). In a biological framework – also occupied, again, by James – a novel is like an organism whose shape is determined by its purpose (not the other way round), a purpose that also includes the effect it is designed to have on its readers. The three main 'variables' of the novel are 'subject-matter, structure, and technique', and these 'depend finally on notions of purpose or function or effect' (Booth 1961: 57). In the same way that James refuses to accept any pre-existing, pre-determining ways of writing the novel, and Trilling repudiates Parrington's insistence on political and social relevance, Booth argues that only the novel's purpose within the context of its specific conception can define and shape its form and content.

This sense of the limitless possibilities of novels restricted only by their initial choice of subject seems to correspond with Trilling's celebration of the variety to which the form gives rise. But Booth sees Trilling's recommendation of the 'novel of ideas' in *The Liberal Imagination* as an example of exactly the kind of extraneous constriction, or 'normative' approach, he wants to resist in favour of being 'descriptive' (Booth 1961: 31). There is an incoherence here, however, that comes close to wrecking the whole edifice of *The Rhetoric of Fiction*, and to which we shall return at the end of the book. Booth is close to rejecting rules established elsewhere in order to smuggle in his own. 'The ultimate problem in the rhetoric of fiction', he asserts, is 'that of deciding for whom the author should write' (1961: 396). But regardless of whether he writes for his peers, or fellow-novelists, 'himself as imagined reader', or his wider audience (1961: 397), he is involved in an act of communication that cannot be other than moral because, again, the human activity of communication can only ever be a moral act; one available, that is, for approval or condemnation.

DESCRIPTIVE AND NORMATIVE CRITICISM

Descriptive criticism is concerned only with what is there, not with what ought to be there according to some pre-existing norm, or set of rules. Normative criticism, on the other hand, evaluates particular novels on the basis of whether or not they meet norms held by the critic, or more generally, by a community of critics and society at large. Walter Besant takes a normative approach to the novel, and Henry James a descriptive.

Towards the end of *The Rhetoric of Fiction*, the approach hardens into the normative view that technical innovation should always be subordinate to the 'obligation to be as clear about' the 'moral position' as possible (1961: 389). It seems at this point as if Booth is much more interested in a 'conscious moral purpose' (James 1884: 62) for the novel than either James or Trilling.

Booth is certainly a long way here from Trilling's commitment to the liberating potential of ambiguity. Although he shared a belief in the need for novels to conduct a complex investigation of the disparities between illusion and reality, he had a firm view of the moral certainties such an investigation ought to yield. 'Pure' narration has 'fouled' our 'lines of communication': 'we have looked for so long at foggy landscapes reflected in misty mirrors that we have come to *like* fog' (Booth 1961: 372). The task of the novel, as Booth insists on it, is not to create the fog but to issue fog warnings. The 'deliberate confusion' of 'fundamental truths' (1961: 285) ought not to be the purpose of the novel.

SUMMARY

Henry James wrote 'The Art of Fiction' to counter normative approaches to the novel and to argue that the creative use of freedom was precisely what could make the novel into an art form. Novels should be judged not by the subject they settle on, but on how they treat it. He deployed the concept of 'organic form' to argue that subjects entailed their own most appropriate treatment. Three questions were crucial for James: Is the treatment appropriate to the subject? Is the novel unified, preferably by the construction of some central perspective? Has the writer managed to fuse a representation of the world with his own impressions, or imagination, so that not 'reality' but the 'illusion of reality' is there to be admired? For Trilling, the novel is not merely a form of art but the means by which political dogmatism can be opposed. The novel should be concerned not with fixing an image of society for the reader to condemn, with realism simply, but with the 'question of realism', with probing the limitations of conventional representations and penetrating through to the world beyond surface illusions. The novel, because of that openness James identified and celebrated, is the perfect vehicle for renovating the individual will so that the self compromised by society and dogmatic politics can discover its potentiality. Booth, like James and Trilling, repudiates the imposition of external rules on the novel. But his insistence on the novel as an act of communication entails the firm belief that moral clarity should be its principal aim. The distinction between 'pure' and 'impure' narration is, in the end, only a distinction between 'covert' and 'overt' rhetoric, for Booth. He is convinced that an insistence on this distinction has resulted in so much fog that readers have grown to like and value it. All three writers see 'freedom' and 'morality' as vital to the novel. But what they mean by those terms is the issue.

2

REALISM AND REPRESENTATION

Since the ascendance of the modern novel as a literary form in the seventeenth and eighteenth centuries, discussions about its merits have been closely connected with questions of realism and representation. As Booth argues, the 'assumption that a novel should seem real' (1961: 53) has been around since its inception. James, Trilling, and Booth certainly share this assumption. The aim of this chapter is to examine the diverse theories of these three writers, notwithstanding their common basis, on realism and representation.

JAMES, THE NEW YORK EDITION PREFACES, AND THE 'FATAL FUTILITY OF FACT'

James is committed, as we saw in Chapter 1, not to 'reality' but to the 'air of reality' (James 1884: 53). The task of the novel is to create an intense illusion of the real. His interest, then, was in the artful representation of his material and not in some kind of documentary inclusiveness for its own sake. When the Scottish writer Robert Louis Stevenson (1850–94) responded to 'The Art of Fiction', he objected to James's claim that the novel 'competes with life' (James 1884: 53): '[n]o art is true in this sense: none can 'compete with life': not even history, built indeed of indisputable facts'. Only 'experience itself, in the cockpit of life, can torture and slay' (Stevenson 1884:

REALISM AND REPRESENTATION

By contrast with the 'romance' – with its emphasis on adventure, fantasy, and the unreal – 'realism' can broadly be seen as involving a commitment to depicting ordinary life in faithful ways. But what counts as 'ordinary life' and a 'faithful' depiction of the 'real' is subject to shifting senses of the 'ordinary', conflicting conventions of depiction, and changing views of what the 'real' is. Whereas, for example, Balzac devoted a lot of energy to describing the streets of Paris and detailing exactly what his characters were wearing, the English novelist Virginia Woolf (1882–1941) believed that real life was 'within' (Allott 1959: 77), and that the goal should be psychological realism. For the three critics under consideration here, there is a tension between realism and representation. Although the words are often used interchangeably, the difference between the two becomes more apparent if we think of 'representation' as 're-presentation'. The use of 'representation', as distinct from 'realism', is an acknowledgement of the extent to which what is real in a novel can only ever be an illusion of the real: that is, a product of the novelist's skills of selection and invention.

918). But James was as wary of the 'fatal futility of Fact' (James 1907–9: 1140) in his early reviews of the novels of Anthony Trollope (1815–82) as he was in a later essay on the work of the Frenchman, Émile Zola (1840–1902).

Dwelling on the account of a 'shabby dinner party' in Trollope's *Miss Mackenzie* (1865), James concedes that '[i]t is as well described as it possibly could be' but that it 'possesses no interest but such as resides in the crude facts'. The 'picture is clever', and 'it is faithful', but 'it is not interesting' (1865: 1315). Similarly, Trollope is praised for being a 'good observer' in *The Belton Estate* (1866), but condemned for being 'literally nothing else' (James 1866b: 1326). Zola took the approach of a scientist, or social scientist, to novels. Realism, for Zola, meant the inclusion of the seamier side of life, especially when it came to sex, prostitution, and the like. This is certainly the case in *Nana*, a novel that James reviewed in 1880, the year of its publication. Partly with the sensitivity of some of his American readers in mind, James described the novel as possessing 'monstrous uncleanness' (1880: 865).

What James seems to be objecting to, however, is less the putative immorality of the novel, more the lack of taste that has resulted in such indiscriminate inclusiveness. The novel can be crammed with facts and detailed descriptions in an attempt minutely to represent the real world. But much more is necessary for it to be a work of art. James considers this at length in his prefaces to the New York edition (1907–9) of his novels and tales.

In the early twentieth century, James set about revising a selection of his novels and tales for 'The Novels and Tales of Henry James: New York Edition'. In all, twenty-four volumes were published and a preface was written for each. In 1934, the American critic Richard P. Blackmur collected these prefaces under the title, *The Art of the Novel*; and this has often been erroneously taken as James's own volume. James never gathered the prefaces together in this way, although it did cross his mind to do so. To his fellow American novelist W. D. Howells (1837–1920), he wrote:

> They ought, collected together . . . to form a sort of comprehensive manual . . . for aspirants in our arduous profession. Still, it will be long before I shall want to collect them together for that purpose and furnish *them* with a final Preface.

> (James 1908: 254)

James did not offer the prefaces as his systematic account of the novel; they are more an analysis of his own compositional methods in the form of what one reviewer called 'auto-criticism' (Schuyler 1908: 104).

In a shrewd analysis of James's prefaces in relation to realism, Booth helps us to see why James believed that a simple devotion to facts was unhealthy for Trollope and Zola, and for the novel in general. Booth argues (1961: 42) that 'intensity' is at the centre of James's realism. The intensity, that is, of an illusion of the real. To try for the real, as Trollope and Zola appeared to be doing, was to confuse art and life. Life may be an affair of the real, but there can only be an illusion of the real in novels. The novel represents, rather than presents, the world, and the trick is to conceal this from the reader where possible. James described life as 'all inclusion and confusion' and art as 'all discrimination and selection' (1907–9: 1138); 'life has no direct sense whatever for the subject' (1907–9: 1139).

We are back here with James's concentration on the importance of the subject, the character or anecdote that has given rise to the novel in the first place, and the need to develop 'the logic of the particular case' (1907–9: 1139). Before writing *The Princess Casamassima* (1886), one of his most socially dense novels, James roamed around the streets of London allowing himself to be bombarded with people and impressions. Unlike Zola – or James's sense of what he does, at least – James did not see it as his business to incorporate as much of the city as possible into his novel. To 'a mind curious, before the human scene', '[p]ossible stories' and 'presentable figures' emerge as 'perception and attention' begin to 'light our steps' (1907–9: 1086).

The novelist at a 'particular *window*' (James 1890a: 65) frames the scene: what is left out is at least as important as what is included and, as we shall see in Chapter 4, the angle of vision the window offers is crucial to the story being told. Neither Trollope nor Zola gave James any sense of a window: they presented pictures 'without composition', or presided over the 'large loose baggy monsters' (1907–9: 1107) for which James berated Tolstoy. James scorns the idea that such monsters are more life-like than novels artistically conceived and artfully produced; and he invokes in the process that principle of organic form we discussed in Chapter 1:

> We have heard it maintained, we well remember, that such things are 'superior to art'; but we understand least of all what *that* may mean . . . There is life and life, and as waste is only life sacrificed and thereby prevented from 'counting', I delight in a deep-breathing economy and an organic form.
>
> (1907–9: 1107–8)

Once again, fiction competes with life. A novel that includes as much life as Tolstoy's *War and Peace* (1863–9) misses the point: such an onslaught on the real will result only in waste and lifelessness. To be life-like, novels (like bodies) need to be carefully organized and good at excreting waste.

Surely, though, Tolstoy, Trollope, and Zola, would have argued that their novels were slices of life, full-blooded, and real, as distinct from James's contrivances? James confronted this view directly in one of his last essays, 'The New Novel' (1914). 'How can a slice of life', he argues

The phrase 'slice of life' is a direct translation of the French *tranche de la vie*. It was first used in connection with realism by the playwright Jean Jullien (1854–1919). It implies that novels can be unmediated, all-inclusive, presentations of the real world. James is reacting in his preface (1907: 1107–8) to Matthew Arnold's observation that 'we are not to take *Anna Karenina* as a work of art; we are to take it as a piece of life' (1887: 457).

with great acuity, 'be anything but illustrational of the loaf' (1914: 271–2)? There is 'no such thing as an amorphous slice'. It is idle to bask in the easy consolations to realism seemingly offered by the 'slice of life' method, for the 'idea of choice and comparison' arises from the moment an author wields his knife (1914: 271). Returning to the question of facts and how they can hinder rather than foster an illusion of realism, James attacks the English novelist Arnold Bennett's *Clayhanger* for its 'dense . . . array' of facts and lack of any 'interest' at the centre. For James, interest on life accrues in the novel rather as it does on capital in a bank. The author invests his subject in the bank of his imagination and produces an imaginative sense of its centre of interest in the shape of novels that are never realistic, but can only *appear* to be realistic. Another way of putting this is to say that the author's experience of the real world appreciates in value once he exercises his imagination on it. The 'affair of the painter is not the immediate, it is the reflected field of life, the realm . . . of *appreciation*'. James's 'interest' in his story arises in this process of 'appreciating' or capitalizing on its value (James 1907–9: 1091).

Booth and James appear to agree, then, on the need for novels to represent the world in seemingly real ways. But they part company when it comes to the question of 'dissimulation' (Booth 1961: 44) or trickery. In his preface to *The American* (a novel first published in 1877), James made a distinction between 'romance', which has only a limited responsibility to the 'real', and 'realism' in terms of the 'balloon of experience' which is 'tied to the earth' so that 'we know where we are' (1907–9: 1064). The 'real represents to my perception the things we cannot possibly *not* know', even though 'particular instances' of the real may not yet have 'come our way'. The 'romantic stands', on the other hand, for things 'we never *can* directly know' (1907–9: 1062–3). Readers have a 'general sense of the way things happen' and tend to cling fairly tenaciously to the rope connecting fiction with the world. To achieve an illusion of the real in a novel, 'the way things don't happen may be artfully made to pass for the way things do' (1907–9: 1065).

Whatever ambitions towards the real a novel entertains, it always involves selection, re-arrangement, and the distortion of the chaos of life into plots, or whatever. As the novelist Ivy Compton-Burnett (1888–1969) wryly observed: 'As regards plots I find real life no help at all. Real life seems to have no plots. And as I think a plot desirable and almost necessary, I have this extra grudge against life' (1945: 249).

The reader's sense of how things usually happen is allied to a sense of 'reflexion and criticism' that must be 'successfully drugged' (1907–9: 1065) if an illusion of the real is to be projected. Life may lack unity, or a centre of interest, but without these the novel is worthless for James. There was no end to the drugs, or narrative methods, James felt able to apply in order to distract his readers from the actual distance between his novels and the real world.

THE QUESTION OF REALISM IN TRILLING'S *BEYOND CULTURE* AND *THE OPPOSING SELF*

As we saw in the last chapter, the emphasis in *The Liberal Imagination* is on the extent to which novels ought to question reality and its representation. In *Beyond Culture*, Trilling suggests that even novels that oppose the dominant culture by challenging simplifying views of representation do 'not always tell the truth or the best kind of truth' (Trilling 1965: viii): their anti-social positions can too easily be socialized as they are read and studied within an institutional critical and academic framework that leads to the 'legitimization of the subversive' (1965: 23). When studied in an academic environment, even the most disturbing novel can simply turn into an object of 'habitual regard' (1965: 9), becoming 'static and commemorative' rather than 'mobile and aggressive' (1965: 11). The need, then, is to recognize that there is a realm beyond culture and its representation; a realm which the reader must occupy from time to time if he or she is not to be rendered

CULTURE

For Matthew Arnold (1822–88) in his *Culture and Anarchy* (1869), culture is 'a pursuit of our total perfection by means of getting to know, on all the matters which most concern us, the best which has been thought and said in the world; and through this knowledge, turning a stream of fresh and free thought upon our stock notions and habits' (Arnold 1869: 6). This formulation, especially its emphasis on reinvigorating our 'stock notions and habits', neatly describes much of Trilling's agenda as a critic. In a way related to Arnold's definition, culture has often been taken to denote high art: the literature, music, and painting, for example, which appeal only to the few. We have now become familiar, however, with phrases such as 'mass culture' and 'popular culture', as well as with 'low culture'. More widely, culture is the antithesis of what is natural and gathers together all those forms of behaviour that distinguish, where they do, human beings from other forms of life. In *The Opposing Self*, Trilling argues that 'culture' is 'the word by which we refer not only to a people's achieved work of intellect and imagination but also to its mere assumptions and unformulated valuations, to its habits, its manners, and its superstitions' (1955b: ii). Culture is defined, in *Sincerity and Authenticity*, as 'a unitary complex of interacting assumptions, modes of thought, habits, and styles, which are connected in secret as well as overt ways with the practical arrangements of a society and which, because they are not brought to consciousness, are unopposed in their influence over men's minds' (Trilling 1972: 125). This might also serve as a definition of 'ideology'. The role of the novel, in part, should be to make this culture conscious to a self who can then oppose it. For Trilling, as one critic puts it, the novel is 'less a *pillar* of society', more its '*questioner*' (Holloway 1973: 337).

impotent by that culture. Trilling's belief in the value of this region arises in part from his uneasy situation in a university setting (which is discussed in the introductory chapter).

For Trilling in *Beyond Culture*, that realm is constituted by Sigmund Freud's (1856–1939) 'primal, non-ethical energies' (Trilling 1965: 17). Trilling wants to hang on to the notion he sees in Freud of the self as a 'biological fact' (Trilling 1965: 97):

We reflect that somewhere in the child, somewhere in the adult, there is a hard, irreducible, stubborn core of biological urgency, and biological necessity, and biological *reason*, that culture cannot reach and that reserves the right, which sooner or later it will exercise, to judge the culture and resist and revise it.

(1965: 99)

It is from this kind of vantage-point that novels, and what they represent, can be interrogated. Whereas James was committed to concealing the boundary between the text and the world, Trilling's interest was often in making it more conspicuous so that what is materially beyond culture, as in the biological self posited by Freud, could be used to critique and renovate that culture without being absorbed by it. For Trilling, novels cannot be realistic; rather, they propose a relation between themselves and reality. This idea is at the root of Trilling's objection to novels that offer a (Marxist) critique of society based on an unproblematic sense of reality and its representation. He approved of novels that 'tended to see reality as an ambiguous fabric' (Reising 1986: 96). In a related way, he thought that to forget that one is reading a story (a forgetfulness that James usually strives for), is to become 'absorbed', uncritical, and passive in the presence of coercive culture:

FREUD AND PRIMAL URGES

For Freud, the social self is a product of necessary but costly civilizing processes. The 'unconscious' urges of the pre-social self, including its sexual impulses and desires, are repressed as part of the means by which that social self is produced. These continue to be more or less successfully controlled by the 'ego', the rational sector of the self distilled from the unconscious, amoral, 'id'. Trilling believes that the novel, and culture generally, often participates in a civilizing distortion of the self. This requires regular inspection and correction so that culture can maintain its oppositional energies. Trilling's most concise account of Freud and culture is in his Freud Anniversary Lecture, *Freud and the Crisis of Our Culture* (1955a).

> To know a story when we see one, to know it *for* a story, to know that it is not reality itself but that it has a clear and effective relation with reality – this is one of the great disciplines of the mind.
>
> (Trilling 1950: 254)

An uncritical adherence to realism, then, as Booth would agree for different reasons, blurs the distance between novels and the world that James was both keen to preserve and anxious to conceal within the meshes of his illusions. We now need to consider the bearing of all this on Trilling's attitudes towards realism and representation in *The Opposing Self*.

The connection between *Beyond Culture* and *The Opposing Self* is clear from the very title of the latter. *The Opposing Self* is a sequence of nine essays that focus mainly on the novel. Most relevant to our purposes here are the discussions of Dickens's *Little Dorrit* (1855–7), Tolstoy's *Anna Karenina* (1874–6), Jane Austen's *Mansfield Park* (1814), and an essay on the American novelist William Dean Howells. For *The Liberal Imagination*, political dogmatism (especially Marxism) is the novel's biggest enemy; in *The Opposing Self* it is the compromising pressures of culture. In ways that anticipate the argument of both *Beyond Culture* and *Sincerity and Authenticity*, Trilling contends that the 'modern self, like Little Dorrit', in Dickens's novel of that name, 'was born in a prison' (Trilling 1955b: ii). In the middle of what many commentators regard as one of the most conservative and reactionary decades in American history (see the introductory chapter), Trilling offers the novel as a vehicle of 'autonomy and delight, of surprise and elevation, of selves conceived in opposition to the general culture' (1955b: vi).

The 'biological fact' of the self in *Beyond Culture* corresponds with Trilling's cautious commitment to a 'literalism' in *The Opposing Self* (1955b: 84) which James would have found difficult in accepting. Trilling considers the extent to which, for some critics, *Little Dorrit* is unrealistic because it is too schematic a novel; it relies too heavily, that is, on 'pattern', 'generalization', and 'abstraction' (Trilling 1955b: 57). But in keeping with his advocacy in *The Liberal Imagination* of the flexibility of the novel form, he is keen to release fiction from the stranglehold of realism by arguing that 'the novel at its best is only incidentally realistic' (1955b: 57). Trilling makes an interesting move, though, when examining the symbolism of the prison in the novel. The prison owes its force as a symbol to the fact that it is an 'actuality before it is ever a symbol'. Its 'connection' with the 'will', stifled everywhere in the novel, is 'real', it 'is the practical negation of man's will which the will of society has contrived' (1955b: 46). For Trilling, we need to remember that Dickens knew about prisons, and that he had been in one as a child when his father was arrested for debt. Only when we have confronted these hard facts are we in a position to consider the less palpable, metaphorical dimensions of the prison.

In *The Opposing Self*, Trilling observed that his students often found it difficult to realize that characters spend money in novels (1955b: 82). At the expense of the literal, concrete levels at which many novels work, they saw everything as merely representative of something else. The tendency of all critics, not just students, is to concentrate on con-notations (or associations) rather than denotations. Whatever forms of representation and realism are in play for Trilling, however, they always exist in relation to, and in dialogue with, manifestations of the literal, or what he described as 'the familial commonplace . . . the materiality and concreteness by which it exists, the hardness of the cash and the hardness of getting it, the inelegance and intractability of family things' (quoted in Rodden 1999: 356–7).

Trilling is bored with the 'bourgeois reality' (1955b: 80) of William Dean Howells's world and the 'elaborate hoax' (1955b: 79) of the family it revolves around. His precise objection, however, is to the idealization of the family, and to the extent to which Howells's novels seem to elevate the actual, or the ordinary, into being 'typical, formal, and *representative*' (Trilling 1955b: 82). Once again, his appeal is to the importance of the actual, the literal. Lost in Howells is 'the literality of matter, the peculiar authenticity and authority of the merely deno-tative' (Trilling 1955b: 82). Plot manipulations are a way of 'escaping

DENOTATION

Where a word, sentence, or section of a novel 'denotes' there is a literal relation of the most direct and simple kind between it and the aspect of experience or society to which it refers. 'Red', for example, denotes the name of a colour; its connotations may include danger, prostitution, and so on.

from reality' rather than representing it. Trilling's preference, which he saw as widespread among critics and literary scholars, is for the 'abstract and conceptual' (1955b: 83); in a similar way, we are mostly happy that the chaos of the biological self is held off by culture. But if culture depends on the periodic renovations of the opposing self, correspondingly, 'there still is a thing that we persist in calling "literal reality", and we recognize in works of art a greater or less approximation to it' (1955b: 83). Trilling deplores Howell's 'extravagance of literalism' and his denial of the importance of 'form' (1955b: 84). But he rejects the idea that form can be supremely important: there can be neither novels nor form without 'matter in its sheer literalness, in its stubborn denotativeness' (1955b: 85).

Tolstoy's *Anna Karenina*, as Arnold with his 'piece of life' acknowledged (see p. 43), became the standard in the nineteenth century for the realistic novel. It was often confused with the turbulent life and history it sought to represent. But Trilling pursues the extent to which Tolstoy's realism, as James well knew, is as much an affair of omissions as of inclusions. Tolstoy gives his readers 'not reality itself but a sort of idyll of reality' (Trilling 1955b: 62). This idyll is constructed by leaving out 'evil' (1955b: 62); yet evil, for Trilling, is 'the very essence of reality' (1955b: 89). What Tolstoy 'has done is to constitute as reality the judgment which every decent, reasonably honest person is likely to make of himself'. In other words, Tolstoy's 'reality is not objective at all', it 'is the product of his will and desire' (Trilling 1955b: 61). It succeeds as a novel mostly where we see the 'spirit of man' at 'the mercy of the actual and trivial' (1955b: 65). Realistic novels, then, cannot avoid the dissimulations they pretend to abhor and which James celebrated. However credulous Trilling is about the neutral appearance of the actual in novels – they can only be actual in a so-to-speak kind of way – his insistence on their therapeutic presence is an intriguing feature of his theory of realism.

In his account of *Mansfield Park*, Lady Bertram is presented as the stubborn matter, or biological fact, that interrogates falsifying representation and, by extension, the trickery of realism. It is one of Trilling's most original and inspired critical moments. Novels, like the theatre, offer 'the experience of the diversification of the self' (1955b: 193). Indeed, the amateur theatricals at the heart of *Mansfield Park* dramatize this very issue. For Jane Austen, representation is at the core of 'personality' (Trilling 1955b: 202): the skill of representation, the

DEATH INSTINCT

In *Beyond the Pleasure Principle* (1920), Freud argues that the 'aim of all life is death', and that as 'inanimate things existed before living ones', the 'instinct to return to the inanimate state' is universal. He anchors this instinct in (pre-cultural) biological history. It is part of 'the tension which . . . arose in what had hitherto been an inanimate substance endeavouring to cancel itself out. In this way the first instinct came into being: the instinct to return to the inanimate state' (1920: 311).

appearance of sincerity being its principal achievement, is what allows the 'personality' to develop from 'character'. The personality is a theatrical event, whereas character is the refusal of such a process. This is to be the great theme of *Sincerity and Authenticity*. The refusal of personality, the desire to revert to matter, or to the 'biological fact' of the self (which Trilling equates with Freud's account of the 'death instinct' in *Beyond Culture*), is one of our 'secret inexpressible hopes' (1955b: 202). Literalism, or stubborn denotation, battles with the compromising pressure of realism on the real in the novel. It lurks in fiction as a version of our biological self, with its powers of cultural resistance. In *Mansfield Park*, it is embodied in an inert Lady Bertram, who occupies the sofa, surrounded by moral turmoil and feverish representations as she seeks 'to escape from the requirements of personality' (Trilling 1955b: 200) in the interests of preserving 'the integrity of the self' (1955b: 197). Indolence, the refusal to act or become involved, amounts to a vigorously resistant selfhood. The relation between integrity and realism is also at the centre of Booth's *The Rhetoric of Fiction*.

REALISM IN *THE RHETORIC OF FICTION*

Early in *The Rhetoric of Fiction*, Booth considers the idea that the difference between the 'intrinsic and extrinsic' is central to any definition of realism in fiction (Booth 1961: 93). As we discussed in Chapter 1, by rhetoric Booth means the devices used by an author as part of that act of communication, or persuasion, which he sees as constituting all novels. 'Extrinsic rhetoric' is one way of labelling the overt commentary of conspicuous narrators. Where the narrator is much less conspicuous, or even seemingly invisible, judgements about the characters and issues involved are intrinsic to the novel, or embedded (for example) in the scenes between characters. Partly on the authority of Aristotle, no less, the New Critics, in particular, tended to castigate the extrinsic approach as impure, or unrealistic, and to celebrate the intrinsic, on the other hand, as being pure and realistic.

Plato made an important distinction, further pursued by Aristotle, between 'simple narrative' (or 'diegesis') and 'narrative conveyed by imitation (*mimesis*)' (Plato 1972: 60) which does indeed, at first sight, appear to correspond with that between the extrinsic and the intrinsic. Furthermore, Aristotle seems to favour the intrinsic approach over the extrinsic when drawing on Plato's terminology. He praises Homer for speaking in his own person 'as little as possible' (Aristotle 1972: 125) and for avoiding, thereby, too many elements extraneous to the imitated action. Booth sees this dispute as central to the consideration of realism in the novel. But before turning to it, he offers a useful taxonomy, or list, of the elements involved in the concept of realism itself. Booth proposes that there are three variables, three areas over which any author has to exercise control, in producing the effect of realism: subject-matter, structure, and narrative technique.

The subject-matter can involve a commitment to doing 'justice to reality outside the book', or to society (reverting to the narrative model on p. 16), or 'social reality' (Booth 1961: 55). When Trilling concentrates on the representation of Lady Bertram's integrity to the self in *Mansfield Park*, Booth would term this 'metaphysical' reality or 'truth' (1961: 55). Some writers regard their subject-matter as the 'sensations' aroused by objects and people in the world of experience, the task being the 'accurate transcription' (1961: 56) of such sensations. Finally – although Booth admits that he is passing over, among

DIEGESIS AND MIMESIS

Diegesis is narration, or direct story-telling, whereas mimesis is the imitation of an action, or of what Aristotle calls 'people doing things' (1972: 92). The apparent opposition, which Booth ultimately denies, between telling and showing descends from Plato and Aristotle.

many others, 'economic, psychological', and 'political' (1961: 56) programmes – there is the broad subject-matter of character and how much of any particular character should be included, or described, and how, for the purposes of realism.

Writers who 'have tried to make their *subjects* real' usually seek 'a realistic *structure* or shape of events' (1961: 56). The key issue here is that of probability in relation to cause and effect. Some novelists have concluded that it is 'unrealistic to show chance at work' in what readers always know is actually a 'fictional world', whereas others reject 'a careful chain of cause and effect' (1961: 56) as artificial. If life-likeness is to be a gauge of realism, the 'soaring climaxes or clear and direct opening expositions', in fact plots in general, are to be 'deplored' (1961: 56).

It is narrative technique, however, that takes Booth back to the main object of his attack: the privileging of the intrinsic over the extrinsic in the interests, mistakenly, of realism. Where a novel veers towards focusing on the metaphysical, technical dogmatism is likely to be the result. A writer dealing with the ambiguities of the human condition, the lack of certainty about anything in the world, for example, is likely to insist on the exclusion of the 'authoritative narrative techniques' (1961: 56) of the extrinsic method. Whereas this kind of realism often results in 'creating the illusion that the events are taking place unmedi-ated by the author' (1961: 57), other writers require that stories should be told as they 'might be told in real life' (1961: 57). Joseph Conrad's (1857–1924) *The Heart of Darkness* (1902) would be a case in point, even though there can be nothing realistic about the phenomenal powers of recall and narrative control with which Conrad imbues Marlow.

Booth believes that it is important to bear in mind the different agendas of writers who think that realism is an end in itself and those who see it as the means towards some other end. There are openly didactic writers for whom realism is only the means by which their particular message is transmitted; such writers are likely to fracture the illusion of realism where necessary. An example of this would be the constant interruption of the story by George Eliot's narrator in *Middlemarch* (1871–2). For Henry James, Booth argues, the illusion of realism, rather than realism itself, is the objective. The creation of this illusion 'as an effect to be realized in the reader' (1961: 58) is subord-inate to all other considerations. A writer such as Dickens may have prided himself on his mimesis, his relentless imitations of action (although he often included narrative asides), but he was always willing to sacrifice realism for the sake of comic effect or entertainment.

Like James and Trilling, Booth is vigorously opposed to prescriptions in advance about realism. Booth sees James as committed to that 'dissimulation' discussed in the first section of this chapter. Yet James certainly did not have a one-size-fits-all narrative strategy. In a nutshell, Booth's position is that there should not be 'a general rhetoric in the service of realism', but 'a particular rhetoric for the most intense experience of distinctive effects' (1961: 50). Horses for courses, we might say. In the same way that Aristotle did not rule out diegesis, objecting only to its excessive use, Booth argues that extraneous commentary may be necessary for the sake of clarity and clarification in some narrative situations, but obtrusive and unwelcome in others. This takes us back not only to the concept of organic form, but to one of its first proponents, Aristotle. The unity of a text was critical for Aristotle. As a biologist, his model for that unity was the body. Plays in particular, which is what he had in mind in his *Poetics*, should represent, or imitate, a 'unified action', so that they produce their 'proper pleasure like a single whole living creature' (Aristotle 1972: 123). The point about bodies, or organisms, however, is not just that they are organized, but that they are organized for diverse purposes and can adapt, physically and mentally, to particular environments.

There are few, if any, rules that can be handed down in advance for the unique experiences an individual encounters. The same goes for the novel. The blanket rule that the intrinsic method will always serve the purposes of realism better is absurd: it implies that realism (in ways that Booth's taxonomy has falsified) is a monolithic category and overlooks the extent to which communication, again the main purpose of the novel for Booth, should have as its goal successful transmission and reception in particular contexts. For Booth, every element of the narrative model on p. 16 is part of this overall transaction. But as we saw at the end of the last chapter, Booth's flexibility is a form of the dissimulation of which he accuses James. By the end of *The Rhetoric of Fiction*, as will emerge in the final chapter, it is clear that Booth prefers the extrinsic to the intrinsic method, even though he wants to deny the validity of the distinction. This is why he attacks James for wanting to conceal the illusory nature of his realism.

SUMMARY

One way of thinking about the issues raised in this chapter is to hook them on to the notion of integrity. James devoted a lot of energy to the illusion of reality and its achievement in fiction. Paradoxically, he wanted to transmit that sense of illusion without dispelling it, and this is one of the functions of his prefaces. The integrity of the subject had to be respected above all, however, and the test of this was in whether its treatment was appropriate to it. James saw himself as the supreme judge of all this, and certainly not other readers and critics and the rules to which they might adhere. Trilling's emphasis is on the extent to which realism is always a form of representation distinct from the real. He saw pattern, symbolism, the shaping of events in plots, and the like, as essential to good novels. But he also hankered after the presence of the literal, the stubborn facts of life that could argue with the forms of representation to which they are being subjected. He saw these facts as versions of the self, or character, that could resist where necessary, and periodically, the distorting forms of the self, known as personalities, that culture has foisted onto the self. The integrity of selfhood, and corresponding presentations of the resisting real, is ultimately much more important to Trilling than realism. For Booth, novels have particular purposes, and the rhetoric they deploy should be determined by those particularities. His overarching focus, however, is on communication. This means that he moves against forms of realism, such as 'pure narrative', that produce the kind of fog discussed at the end of the last chapter. The integrity of the novel as a communication process, as ever, is the framework for Booth's approach to realism.

3

AUTHORS, NARRATORS, AND NARRATION

Wayne C. Booth's most significant contribution to the theory and criticism of prose fiction in *The Rhetoric of Fiction* is his analysis of 'point of view' and the functions of the narrator in relation to the author, text, and reader. For this reason, this chapter is organized rather differently from the rest in that the principal focus will be on Booth. James and Trilling will figure from time to time, but the discussion of James and the point of view, which is bound up with his ideas about consciousness and the novel, will take place in the next chapter. Trilling has a number of important things to say about narration and point of view, and these will be considered as we go along, but narrative method was not one of his major concerns. After reading this chapter, you will not only have a firm grasp of Booth's way of thinking about narrative, but will also have a set of terms that can usefully be applied to the reading of fiction. Please bear in mind, however, that what follows is a guide to Booth's analysis of narrative method. In the end, not least because of the large number of examples he supplies, my aim is to encourage you to read *The Rhetoric of Fiction* itself.

As we have seen, Booth's constant emphasis is on the novel as an act of communication. For Booth, every novel has a set of values, a way of thinking about the world and morality, which it advocates. Good novels are unambiguous about the values being communicated; where there is ambiguity, because the narrative method is confusing,

POINT OF VIEW

The phrase 'point of view' originally applied to the perspective from which we look at what is depicted in a painting. The artist might arrange the scene, for example, so that we are looking up towards the top of a mountain, or down into a valley. As Friedman argues, it 'has become one of the main concerns' of any novel theorist (1975: 134). By the end of the nineteenth century, it had been extended to fiction to mean the aspects from which the events of the story are regarded or narrated. The use of this phrase for narrative is often attributed to Henry James: he writes of the need for a 'point of view' restricted to a particular character, for example, in his preface to *The Wings of the Dove* (1907–9: 1297). But the first application of the concept to narrative was probably by a friend of Henry James, the English novelist Violet Paget (1856–1935), who wrote under the name of 'Vernon Lee'. Her account of 'point of view' first appeared in essays written and published in the 1890s, and republished in her *The Handling of Words and Other Studies in Literary Psychology*: 'I have described also that most subtle choice of the literary craftsman: choice of the point of view whence the personages and action of a novel are to be seen' (Lee 1923: 20).

Booth is profoundly unhappy. Fundamentally, Booth's aim in Chapters 6 and 7 of *The Rhetoric of Fiction* ('Types of Narration' and 'The Uses of Reliable Commentary') is to continue his campaign against the idea that any one way of writing a novel can become the rule for writing all others. Specifically, however, his target is impersonal, or pure, narration. He insists that overt commentary on characters, events, and morals, can be as effective and artistic as the alternatives. Henry James would have agreed. James disliked obtrusive narrative commentary; and increasingly, he constructed novels with dramatized narrators, often disguised, who were very much part of the action. But he was concerned about taking this kind of method to extremes. He wrote in 'London Notes' that:

> There is always at the best the author's voice to be kept out. It can be kept out for occasions, it can not be kept out always. The solution therefore is to leave it its function, for it has the supreme one.

(James 1897: 1404)

Similarly, Trilling was anxious about the 'banishment of the author from his books', partly because he felt that this 'reinforced the faceless hostility of the world' (1950: 253). In any event, like Booth he argues that in terms of the author 'we always know who is there by guessing who it is that is kept out' (1950: 254). Booth comes close, despite his aim of avoiding prescriptions, to preferring the direct method for the moral clarity it produces. This emerges as he develops his account of 'dramatized' and 'undramatized' narrators.

DRAMATIZED AND UNDRAMATIZED NARRATORS

Booth begins his chapter on 'Types of Narration' by reminding his readers that the traditional way of thinking about point of view is to identify whether a novel was written in the first or third person and then to assess the 'degree of omniscience' (Booth 1961: 149) involved. He argues that establishing whether the story is in the first (*I*) or third person (*he* or *she*) and working out how much the narrator knows about the characters and events is insufficient. We need to consider whether

DRAMATIZED AND UNDRAMATIZED NARRATORS

There are 'rigorously impersonal' (Booth 1961: 151) stories in which there is no sign of actual story-telling. But most novels are passed through the consciousness of one or more tellers. Where such narrators are given few or no personal characteristics, the reader may have an impression of 'unmediated' (1961: 152) narration. This kind of narration is labelled by Booth as 'undramatized'. Jane Austen's novels, for example, usually have an overarching undramatized narrator. 'Dramatized' narrators, irrespective of whether they take part in or have any effect on the story they are telling, are characters in their own right. 'Disguised narrators' (1961: 152) are dramatized narrators who are not labelled by the author as narrators. Many characters in novels find themselves, at some stage or other, telling stories however indirectly. Booth's identification of dramatized narration, whether disguised or otherwise, has helped critics to spot narration going on where it has previously been ignored.

OMNISCIENCE AND PRIVILEGE

An omniscient narrator is 'all knowing'. Such a narrator freely goes in and out of the minds of all the characters and often fully interprets the significance of the events for the reader. George Eliot's narrator in *Middlemarch* (1871–2) is a classic example of this kind of narrator. But even if the narrator seems to be very much a character in the novel, he or she is a device *in the text* used by the author (*outside the text*, and sometimes dead) for telling the story. Narrators can be 'privileged to know what could not be learned by strictly natural means or limited to realistic vision and inference' (Booth 1961: 160), and the degrees of privilege and restriction involved vary enormously between different novels and even within individual texts. Normal readers cannot enter into the thoughts of others; yet we cheerfully allow authors to construct narrators who penetrate not just one but many minds. These 'inside views' differ in the 'depth and axis of their plunge': they can be 'shallow' or deep, moral rather than psychological (or a combination of the two), and so on (Booth 1961: 163).

the 'narrator is dramatized in his own right' and 'whether his beliefs and characteristics are shared by the author' (1961: 151).

Narrators rarely, if ever, know as much as the author, so Booth prefers the word 'privilege' to 'omniscience'. For James, the way to writing a better story is to restrict the privileges of his narrator-agents; he sees omniscience as other-worldly and associates it with turgid scriptures: 'It seems probable that if we were never bewildered there would never be a story to tell about us; we should partake of the superior nature of the all-knowing immortals whose annals are dreadfully dull', (James 1907–9: 1090). Unlike James, Booth often appears to require his implied authors to be like the God of the Christian Bible: omniscient and omnipotent (all-powerful) dispellers of bewilderment. The exercising of this power in novels, however, can produce works of art as clumsily didactic as some of the books of the Old Testament prophets. Booth's concept of the 'implied author', which we shall consider in detail below, was developed in part to address this problem.

There is little doubt that Booth's preference is for some form of dramatized or undramatized narration, rather than impersonal narrative. It helps us to understand Booth's preferences if we relate the approach of *The Rhetoric of Fiction* to one of the biggest influences on it: Aristotle's *Rhetoric*. Aristotle identified three key means of persuasion: the actual argument, the character of the speaker, and the effect of the argument on the listener or reader. For Booth, as for Aristotle, successful communication in the novel depends in no small measure on 'how the particular qualities of the narrators relate to specific effects' (Booth 1961: 150). Trilling endorses his view when writing on George Orwell: 'what matters most of all is our sense of the man' behind the writing 'who tells the truth' (1955b: 151). The qualities of the narrator are at least as important as what is being narrated if we are to be persuaded into the author's view of the world. Booth pursues the relation between the norms of the narrator and implied author relentlessly in *The Rhetoric of Fiction*. He sees impersonal (and even, at times, undramatized) narration as morally detrimental to the reader because it confuses this relation.

A dramatized narrator can be both the principal (or only) teller of the story and yet fully involved in the events. Marlow in Joseph Conrad's *Heart of Darkness* (1902) may come to mind here. Marlow is the main story-teller, but the story he tells is of his own journey in the Congo. Booth calls these characters 'narrator-agents' and distinguishes them from 'mere observers' who have no effect on the story itself (Booth 1961: 153). An example of a mere observer, who is nevertheless a fairly substantial character in his own right, would be Fielding's narrator in *Tom Jones*. The narrator in that novel chats openly with the reader in the introduction to each section of the novel. He discusses his writing habits, the business of reading, whether the reader is enjoying the novel, and even ejects readers in imaginary disagreements with them. Nevertheless, he takes no part in the story itself. Booth was one of the first critics to formalize the distinction between narrator-agents and observers by focusing on the issue of the extent to

NORMS

Norms are values (moral and social) and standards of behaviour. One of Booth's norms in *The Rhetoric of Fiction*, for example, is that novels should communicate their moral positions clearly.

NARRATOR-AGENTS AND MERE OBSERVERS

Both narrator-agents and mere observers are forms of dramatized narration. Narrator-agents produce some 'measurable effect' (Booth 1961: 153)
on the story, whereas observers do not.

which narrators take part in the story. Narrator-agents can play a
significant part in the story (Marlow again), or their degree of involvement in the actual events can be quite small. Nick Carroway in F. Scott
Fitzgerald's *The Great Gatsby* (1925) is an example of the latter.

James's narrator-agents tend to be more narrators than agents:
his aim was usually to place a 'mind of some sort – in the sense
of a reflecting and colouring medium – in possession of the general
adventure' (James 1907–9: 1093). But James never recommended
relinquishing control over these narrator-agents. His novels often seem
to have heavily disguised narrator-agents as part of a dramatized narrative method. But these agents are often tightly gripped in the respective
vices of more or less carefully concealed undramatized narrators.
Booth's *The Rhetoric of Fiction*, largely because of the new vocabulary
and concepts it evolves, helps us to see the extent to which Percy
Lubbock (among others) and the New Critics misunderstood James's
theory and practice.

NARRATIVE COMMENTARY: SUMMARY AND SCENE

Novels that incorporate narrators who offer an overt commentary on
the characters and events have come under attack not only from proponents of pure fiction, or impersonal narration, but from critics who
believe that this kind of commentary is disruptive. As we saw in the
last chapter, narrative commentary not integrated into the dramatic
action of the novel increasingly came to be regarded in the late nineteenth and early twentieth centuries, and beyond, as inartistic. Booth's
contribution to the debate is to reveal how much of this commentary is going on even when novels appear to be showing rather than
telling and, in any event, to demonstrate the need for and importance
of undramatized summary. He believes that direct narrative summary,

as part of the commentary, can be more effective than dramatic, or scenic presentation, depending on the context. Where the reader needs a perspective on the limited or misguided notions of the characters in the story, Booth argues that narrative summary is vital. James constantly stressed the author's responsibility to the subject he was treating. Booth also thought it important to avoid general rules by asking '[h]ow does *this* comment, portrayed in *this* style, serve or fail to serve *this* structure?' (Booth 1961: 187). But for Booth, rather than for James, decisions about the appropriateness of the narrative method at any given point should further be determined by a clear sense of the intended effect on the reader.

Booth thought it important to emphasize that the 'amount and kind' of commentary in relation to what is summarized and scenically presented does, and should, vary according to the context. He also wanted to distinguish between 'self-conscious narrators' (dramatized or undramatized) who are 'aware of themselves as writers' (the narrator in Fielding's *Tom Jones*, for example) and others who 'seem unaware that they are writing, thinking, speaking, or "reflecting" a

SUMMARY AND SCENE

Booth inherited the distinction between summary (or 'picture') and scene from Henry James and also from Percy Lubbock's (1921) account of James's prefaces to the New York Edition. In his notebooks, James defined scene as the 'march of an action', and as the only 'scheme' he could trust (1987: 167); but his remarks there apply only to his writing of the novel, *What Maisie Knew* (1897). He also saw the necessity for summary, especially when novels have to deal with the 'lapse and accumulation of time' (1897: 1403). In his preface to *The Ambassadors*, James argued for variety, for the regular alternation of the 'scenic' and the 'non-scenic' (1907–9: 1319). He relegated summary there, however, to the role of preparing for scenes in his preface to *The Ambassadors* (1907–9: 1317–18). Despite the fact that James never insisted on any one approach, the New Critics in particular misprized his picture-scene distinction and re-mapped it as telling (summary) and showing (scene). As we have discussed, Booth rejects both the idea that the latter is superior to the former and that telling and showing are separable.

literary work' (Booth 1961: 155). In theory, James was appalled by displays of self-consciousness, condemning Anthony Trollope for taking 'a suicidal satisfaction in reminding the reader that the story he was telling was only, after all, a make-believe' (James 1883: 1343). In his own novels, however, as Tilford (1958) has reminded us, there can be a significant level of this kind of self-consciousness. *The Portrait of a Lady* (1881) is a case in point.

The Rhetoric of Fiction expands our sense of the various functions of narrative commentary. Booth demonstrates that narrators can comment on, and interpret, events and characters. They may make generalizations about the world of the novel and what is outside it, with three aims in mind: 'ornamental' effect (Booth 1961: 155), to persuade the reader to enter into the norms of the fictional world being presented, and as an integral part of the novel's dramatic structure. One of the key tasks of the narrator, and for Booth one often best undertaken by undramatized narrators, is 'to tell the reader about facts' (1961: 169). Booth is always much more certain than either James or Trilling that there are such things. There are 'unlimited' ways of telling readers about the facts: these include setting the scene, explaining the meaning of an event or action, summarizing an event that is too insignificant to render through dialogue, and summarizing the thought-processes of a character (1961: 169). Booth also believes that narrators should be used both to control 'dramatic irony' through 'straight description' and to shape the expectations of the reader so that 'he will not travel burdened with the false hopes and fears held by the characters' (1961: 172–3).

There are a number of other functions of the narrative commentary that Booth prefers to be clear and unambiguously apparent: the shaping of the reader's beliefs (1961: 177); the making of accurate

DRAMATIC IRONY

'Dramatic irony' is when the reader understands the significance of a situation within the plot but the character or characters do not. In Henry James's *The Portrait of a Lady*, for example, the reader knows long before Isabel Archer does that Ralph Touchett persuaded his father to leave her a fortune.

judgements of the characters against the norms of the novel; generalizing the importance beyond the novel itself of what goes on there; and even the manipulation of the reader's moods and emotions. Booth sees these functions as much too important to be left to the chance inferences of particular readers. Booth's advocacy of summary over scene, and of personal rather than impersonal narratives, left him vulnerable to attack from critics who saw this rhetoric as destroying the boundaries between authors and texts, and texts and readers. This brings us to one of Booth's most important contributions to the theory of narrative.

THE IMPLIED AUTHOR

In order to understand the power of Booth's concept of the implied author, it is necessary to return briefly to the New Critical context discussed in 'Why James, Trilling, and Booth'. The New Critics thought that novels, and literary works in general, existed independently of their writers and readers. They wanted, that is, the boundaries they saw as separating the author and reader from the text to be as strong as possible. Their interest was less in context, in all the elements outside the boundary of the text, more in the text itself. The New Critics were similar to the Chicago School (see p. 14) in two important ways: both wanted to resist the pre-eminence of historical and biographical approaches to criticism and to 'restore autonomy', as Trilling expressed it, 'to the work of art' (Trilling 1950: 174). More than ten years before the publication of *The Rhetoric of Fiction* in 1961, Trilling declared that literature is 'closer to rhetoric than we today are willing to admit' (1950: 273). But to perceive texts as rhetorical is to challenge the New Critical fervour for 'self-contain[ment]' (1950: 271). This rhetorical, communicative dimension makes it difficult, Trilling believed, to deal 'with art as if it were a unitary thing', or as 'purely' aesthetic (1950: 271).

What separates the Chicago School and Booth from the New Critics is the devotion of the former to Aristotle, with his emphasis not only on structure but on the rhetorical function of art. If the novel is an act of communication, then it must resemble a message. A message has a sender and at least one receiver, and all three elements interact in the negotiation of meaning. The meaning is not in the message, but a result of the communication process as a whole. It makes no sense to regard messages as autonomous. Yet Aristotle also held (as discussed in the last chapter) that a text should function like a unified, independent organism. Booth's task in *The Rhetoric of Fiction*, to put it simply, was to try to reconcile Aristotle's and his own belief in texts as forms of communication between author and reader with New Critical senses of unity and independence. He did this by distinguishing between the author and the implied author. This allowed him to have his cake and to eat it: the text can be regarded both as an act of communication and as an entity with secure, yet permeable, boundaries.

The concept of the implied author allows Booth to preserve a sense of the novel as a structure with its own boundaries and to locate it in the chain of communication specified on p. 16. The author cannot communicate directly with his readers, not least because he or she may already be dead. If the reader frets over what the author intended, there is the paralysing problem of how he or she is ever going to find

IMPLIED AUTHOR

Booth defined the 'implied author' as the author's 'second self'. Whether or not the narrator is dramatized, the novel 'creates an implicit picture of an author who stands behind the scenes' (Booth 1961: 151). The implied author is always different from the real man or woman who wrote the novel and from the dramatized narrator. Booth calls the real author the 'flesh-and-blood author' in *The Company We Keep* (1988a: 134). He also developed there the concept of the 'career author' (1988a: 150). Once we have read two or more novels by the same flesh-and-blood author, we start to put together an entity of two or more implied authors to form a composite career author who is still not equivalent to the flesh-and-blood author (1988a: 134). If the narrator is wholly undramatized, and there is no reference in the text to an implied author, there is no distinction between this 'implied, undramatized narrator' (1961: 151) and the implied author. We form our sense of the implied author from everything said and done in the text, and from the structure of the novel and its overall arrangement. The narrator is only one element in our compound of the implied author. The norms of the narrator may differ from those of the characters, and those of the implied author.

out what that was if the text itself is not the realization of those intentions. Booth smuggles into the text a version of the author, mostly because he believes that this is the means by which the reader's otherwise faulty impressions can be corrected. The implied author communicates with the reader, even though it all seems a bit like a séance at times; and in an effective novel, he leads the reader by the hand and accompanies her in the difficult journey through what might be the moral maze of the story. This is very much the territory Booth revisits and occupies again in his *The Company We Keep*.

Our 'sense of the implied author' comes not just, or mainly, from any 'explicit commentary', but from 'the kind of tale he chooses to tell' (Booth 1961: 73). This sense also includes 'not only the extractable meanings but also the moral and emotional content of each bit of action and suffering of all of the characters' (1961: 73). The implied author 'chooses, consciously or unconsciously, what we read; we infer him as an ideal, literary, created version of the real man; he is the sum of his own choices' (1961: 74–5).

In an essay on Guy de Maupassant (1850–93), a French writer renowned in particular for his short stories, James discusses Maupassant's introduction to *Pierre et Jean* (1888). Maupassant, in the tradition of Flaubert, advocated the avoidance of 'all complicated explanations, all dissertations upon motives'; stories should be confined 'to making persons and events pass before our eyes' (James 1888a: 530). What Maupassant seeks to remove, then, are all those features of the narrative that Booth groups together under the label of rhetoric. Booth's contention, however, is that every move a novel makes implies an author. James agrees: 'M. de Maupassant is remarkably objective and impersonal, but he would go too far if he were to entertain the belief that he has kept himself out of his books. They speak of him eloquently' (1888a: 532).

Trilling comes up with a similar argument when discussing James Joyce's *The Portrait of the Artist as a Young Man* (1916). At one point, the character Stephen Dedalus says that in fiction: 'The personality of the artist, at first a cry or a cadence or a mood and then a fluid and lambent narrative, finally refines itself out of existence, impersonalizes itself, so to speak' (Joyce 1916: 214). Cleverly, Trilling argues that this impersonality 'is described in quite personal terms'. Impersonality, in fact, was one of Joyce's personality traits; and this is a direct expression of it. If Joyce's aim has been to write an impersonal narrative, he has succeeded only in making the implied author conspicuous. Stephen and the text as a whole are clearly Joyce's 'ambassadors' (Trilling 1957: 286).

RELIABLE AND UNRELIABLE NARRATORS

The concept of the implied author led Booth to produce two further labels so frequently applied that few critics pause to attribute them to *The Rhetoric of Fiction*: 'reliable' and 'unreliable' narrators. Before considering these labels, we need to clarify what Booth meant by 'distance' in narrative. In keeping with his focus on the novel as an act of communication, Booth is intensely interested in the 'implied dialogue among [the implied] author, narrator, the other characters, and the reader' (1961: 155). Booth and Trilling (unlike James) want the reader to be aware not only of this dialogue, but of the variable distances between all the elements of it. Booth thinks that 'aesthetic distance' is important when it comes to shaping the 'sense that we are dealing with an aesthetic object' (1961: 156) but that we should not confuse this distance 'with the equally important effects of personal beliefs and qualities, in author, reader, narrator, and all others in the cast of characters' (1961: 156). Part of Booth's mission is to plot the variable distances between these elements of the narrative and the effects of these variations on the reader. What follows is an attempt to schematize Booth's analysis (1961: 156–9).

Distance is often discussed not only in terms of the reader's degree of involvement and identification with, or sympathy for, the implied 'author, narrators, observers, and other characters'; also crucial are

AESTHETIC DISTANCE

The term 'aesthetic distance' relates to the detachment, or 'disinterest-edness' as Kant expressed it in his *Critique of Judgement* (1790), experienced when a novel is read (or a work of art is contemplated). However involved in a novel the reader becomes, this sense of distance will allow him or her to look at it as a work of art and not to confuse it with the real world.

Schematization of Booth's analysis

the various interactions between all these elements of the narrative (Booth 1961: 158). The narrator might be openly critical, for example, of a character approved of by the implied author. One of the most telling distances is 'that between the fallible or unreliable narrator and the implied author who carries the reader with him in judging the narrator' (1961: 158).

This distinction between reliable and unreliable narrators is often used wrongly. Just because narrators 'indulge in large amounts of incidental irony', and are thus unreliable or 'potentially deceptive' (Booth 1961: 159) at such points, that does not make them unreliable. Similarly, narrators who lie do not necessarily pose a problem for the reader as long as she has a secure sense of the implied author's norms. What defines unreliability for Booth is the extent to which the narrator is mistaken, or assumes qualities that the novel as a whole (as incorporated in the implied author) denies him. Booth uses the example of Huckleberry Finn in Twain's novel of that name (1884) as

RELIABLE AND UNRELIABLE NARRATORS

Booth deems a narrator *reliable* when 'he speaks for or acts in accordance with the norms of the work (which is to say, the implied author's norms)', and *'unreliable* when he does not' (1961: 158–9). There is no distance between the implied author and reliable narrators; unreliable narrators are often at odds with the facts and values of the implied author.

a classic unreliable narrator. Huck is constantly berating himself for being wicked; yet the implied author praises him behind his back, so to speak, not least in the way the plot of the novel vindicates his actions (Booth 1961: 159). There is often no sharp division between reliable and unreliable narrators, just as the degree to which unreliable narrators differ from the norms of the implied author is a variable one. Booth sees unreliable narrators as making heavier demands on the reader than reliable narrators.

Booth's real concerns, however, arise when unreliable narrators are combined with confused and confusing implied authors; when the

IRONY

Irony is popularly taken as meaning the opposite of what is said or written. Ironic statements are more complicated than this implies. It is helpful to bear in mind that the word 'irony' comes from the Greek *eiron*, which means 'mask'. There is always something 'behind' an ironic statement. What is said is different from, rather than merely opposite to, what is meant. In his *The Rhetoric of Irony*, Booth distinguishes between two main types of irony: stable and unstable. Readers can figure out incidental ironies in a text if they can measure what the narrator tells them against their sense of the implied author. Localized unreliability may offer intellectual pleasure and cannot threaten the moral edifice of the novel. Unstable irony arises where a reader knows she has to reject the literal meaning of what is being said but cannot see what to measure such statements against. This is often because the implied author is inconsistent or incoherent.

norms of the novel, that is, are unclear. Such texts lack what Booth calls a point of 'security' (1961: 352). He is fully aware of the fact that many novelists, including Henry James in *The Turn of the Screw*, consider such insecurities to be aesthetically powerful. But he sees such texts as wilfully abandoning their moral obligation to communicate responsibly with the reader. Booth defines rhetoric in his last book as the 'whole range of arts not only of persuasion but also of producing or reducing misunderstanding' (Booth 2004: 10). At the core of his sense of rhetoric, there is the English critic I. A. Richards' (1893–1979) contention that 'rhetoric is the study of misunderstandings and their remedies' (Booth 2004: 7). For James, misunderstanding is the very fuel of fiction.

In *The Rhetoric of Fiction*, as we shall see again in Chapter 6, what comes under attack is the attempt to silence authors in the misguided belief that a better novel will result. When evaluating the Russian writer Anton Chekhov's (1860–1904) short story, 'Enemies', Trilling considers the 'modern theory of fiction, learned in considerable part from Chekhov himself', that 'the events of a story must speak for themselves, without the help of the author's explicit comment'. 'Enemies' is an exception to Chekhov's usual practice, and Trilling finds 'this surrender of the artist's remoteness in favor of a direct communication with the reader refreshing as well as moving' (Trilling 1967: 101). This is very much Booth's position, but with an important difference. Booth was too much of a formalist in the Chicago tradition to allow the author, as distinct from the implied author, into the novel.

SUMMARY

The aim of this chapter has been to supply a survey of Booth's most important concepts in *The Rhetoric of Fiction*. Once again, rhetoric has been crucial. Booth sees narration as rhetorical. It is not just an act of communication, but a form of persuasion. Ultimately, effective novels persuade the reader into considering their norms, even if those norms are later rejected. These norms are embodied in the implied author (the sum of all the elements of a novel, and not just the narrator). Booth developed his implied author partly in order to reconcile his emphasis on the novel as a form of communication with his aesthetic commitment to seeing it as an artistic totality where the boundaries between author, text, and reader are stable. Some narrators share the implied author's norms; others do not. Where the implied author undercuts the narrator by denying the qualities he claims (in terms of knowledge, ability, and the like), Booth calls the narrator unreliable. Booth has no problem with unreliable narrators as such, but he worries about the demands they might place on the reader. What also concerns him is the combination of unreliable narration with insecure and incoherent implied authors.

4

POINTS OF VIEW
AND CENTRES OF
CONSCIOUSNESS

Wayne C. Booth's *The Rhetoric of Fiction* was very much the focus of the previous chapter, and here our main concentration will be on Henry James's prefaces to the New York edition of his work. What connects this chapter with Chapter 3 is the concept of point of view. In fact, one of the best ways of preparing to read it would be to look again at the discussion of point of view on p. 56.

TRILLING AND NEW CRITICISM

On the whole, Trilling distanced himself from formalism and New Criticism, and this is why he occupies only a marginal position in this and the previous chapters. He has much more to say about reading and interpretation and especially about the social and moral responsibilities of the novel. In *The Liberal Imagination*, Trilling wrote that 'the novelist of the next decades will not occupy himself with questions of form' (1950: 255). This is not one of Trilling's happiest predictions: novelists and critics alike were to become obsessed with technical matters in the 1950s and on. Trilling attacks New Criticism, despite saying that he has no wish to 'depreciate form', for 'its conscious preoccupation with' it (1950: 256). As we shall go on to discuss, point of view theory hardened into a dogma not least because of correspondences between James's insistence on the need for novels to have

CONSTRUCTED INFLUENCE

We are used to thinking, and often rather loosely, of the influence of a writer on his contemporaries and successors. By 'constructed influence', I mean the process whereby successors interpret a writer (who when dead, can do little about it, of course) so that he or she becomes exactly the kind of influence they need in order to be able to justify a theory or doctrine. James was an authoritative figure in the world of literature when he died. I would argue that the New Critics benefited from that authority by misreading his prefaces so that, in effect, he could legitimate their approach to literature.

an organic unity (see p. 25) and the New Critical emphasis on the formal autonomy of works of art. But James cannot be held account-able for what we might call a process of 'constructed influence'. Trilling saw the desire for unity and a preoccupation with form as severely limiting New Critical approaches to texts; especially because it exercised a powerful influence on young novelists.

As discussed in Chapter 2, Trilling believed that one of the tasks of the novel was to oppose the conservative, unresisting, elements of culture. But, 'form suggests completeness and the ends tucked in; reso-lution is seen only as all contradictions equated, and although form thus understood has its manifest charm, it will not adequately serve the modern experience' (1950: 256). This critical project, and the novels to which it might give rise, pays insufficient attention to what, in the end, Trilling regarded as being at the root of all our actions: 'emotion' (1950: 256). This recalls Booth's stress on the importance of values and beliefs in the novel. Trilling suggests that the boundaries between society, author, and text, and text, reader, and society, are not as stable as James wants to imagine. With his concept of the implied author, Booth sustained this boundary by thinking of it as a membrane: cell membranes, for example, act as both barriers and selective receivers.

There is much about the scientific, anti-humanist, professional edge to New Criticism that Trilling loathed. He is in good company with

Booth here, especially when he attacks the impact of this kind of analysis on the relationship between reader, text, and implied author. Trilling sneers at the 'modern highly trained literary sensibility' that lacks the capacity to respond to the text (1950: 256). Such critics have been 'too eager to identify ironies, and to point to ambiguities, and to make repeated analyses and interpretations'. This 'interferes with our private and personal relation to the literary work' (Trilling 1965: 163). Booth's approach to theories of the point of view involved, in part, reconnecting them to the human world. The negative, dehumanizing impact of the New Critics not just on Hawthorne, but on James himself, is acknowledged indirectly when Trilling discusses Hawthorne in *The Liberal Imagination*. Whereas Hawthorne drew attention to the 'perspicuity of what he wrote', the 'famous movement of' New '[C]riticism which James could know nothing of', turned him into a 'grave, complex, and difficult' writer (1965: 160–1). In turn, Trilling implies, James's theories of fiction were similarly sterilized by the New Critics. In reality, they team with fecundity.

THREE CENTRAL QUESTIONS

Point of view has been regarded as central to James's theory of the novel ever since his prefaces first appeared in 1907–9. In one of the most comprehensive accounts of point of view in narrative, the American critic Norman Friedman reminds us that 'the New Critics' followed 'Henry James in preferring an objective method of presentation', rather than 'the interfering and summarizing authorial narrator' recuperated by Booth (Friedman 1975: 134). For Friedman and a raft of other critics, James advocated objective narrative; and this principally involved, or so the story goes, his rule that novels should be organized around what one character sees and experiences. Three questions will be central to our discussion: Did James develop a consistent theory of the point of view in narrative? Did he turn this into a rule? Can it be detached from his wider epistemological and moral preoccupations? Our answers to these questions will allow us to compare, from time to time, Booth's approach to narrative in *The Rhetoric of Fiction* with James's in the prefaces. Before turning to these questions, however, it will be useful to examine some of the relevant context within which James wrote his prefaces.

EPISTEMOLOGY

Epistemology is a branch of philosophy that concerns itself with knowledge. Among the questions it asks are: What is knowledge? How can we
distinguish between knowledge and belief? What is knowable? Can there
be certain knowledge? James believed that what we know, and can know,
depends to a large extent on where we are standing, what we see, and
our powers (or lack of them) of perception.

THE CONTEXT OF JAMES'S NEW YORK PREFACES

Nineteenth-century critics of the novel, for the most part, identified
only three ways of telling a story: third-person omniscient narration,
the autobiographical (or first-person) method; and the epistolary form
(novels written in letters). It is worth quoting at length the novelist
Anna Laetitia Barbauld's (1743–1825) perceptive treatment of these
different forms of narrative:

> There are three modes of carrying on a story: the narrative or epic as it may be
> called; in this the author related himself the whole adventure . . . It is the most
> common way. The author . . . is supposed to know every thing; he can reveal
> the secret springs of actions, and let us into events in his own time and manner.
> He can indulge . . . in digressions . . . Another mode is that of memoirs; where
> the subject of the adventures relates his own story . . . It has the advantage of
> the warmth and interest a person may be supposed to feel in his own affairs
> . . . It has a greater air of truth . . . A third way remains, that of *epistolary corres-
> pondence*, carried on between the characters of the novel . . . This method
> unites, in a good measure, the advantages of the other two . . . it makes the
> whole work dramatic, since all the characters speak in their own persons.
>
> (Barbauld 1804: 258–9)

In *The Rhetoric of Fiction*, Booth demonstrates just how much more
is involved in the narrative transaction between author, text, and
reader, than voice and privilege; than simply labelling, that is, these
three methods in this way. But his concept of dramatized narration,
and James's approval of what Booth called dramatic narrative, owes a

great deal to much earlier enthusiasms for novels written in letters. Towards the end of the nineteenth century, a fierce debate arose about the degree to which authors should intrude into their stories. A reaction set in against omniscient narrators in particular. As early as 1877, a writer in the widely read literary journal, the *Westminster Review*, argued that '[w]e do not require to be told that so-and-so is a good man or a witty man; we want to feel his goodness and to hear his wit' (Graham 1965: 124).

The question in part, was whether third-person narrative methods could respond to these pressures. Until Booth's *The Rhetoric of Fiction*, the victory in this debate went largely to the New Critics and all those who had managed to extract from James's prefaces a solution to the problem they also saw at work in the practice of his fiction. Although Percy Lubbock in his massively influential *The Craft of Fiction* (1921) devotes quite a lot of space to James's alternation between scenic and pictorial methods, he is 'opposed to omniscience in general' (Martin 1980: 24); he revels in James's *The Ambassadors* (1903), for reasons that Booth would have abhorred, because 'the novelist pushes his responsibility further and further away from himself' (Lubbock 1921: 147). For Lubbock, James's novels are dramatic; and he slickly converts a description of James's practice into a normative account of point of view:

> the full and unmixed effect of drama is denied to the story that is rightly told from the point of view of one of the actors. But when that point of view is held in the manner I have described, when it is open to the author to withdraw from it silently and to leave the actor to play his part, true drama – or something so like it that it passes for true drama – is always possible.
>
> (1921: 262–3)

The normative dimensions of Lubbock's study of James were seized on with alacrity by a large number of critics. One categorical formulation of the doctrine of the point of view comes, for example, in an anthology of fiction edited by Caroline Gordon and Allen Tate, two prominent New Critics:

> We call it the method of the Central Intelligence after Henry James, who insisted that all the action of a novel should be evaluated by a single superior mind placed in the center of the main dramatic situation.
>
> (Gordon and Tate 1950: 444)

Even more emphatically, in a book bravely entitled *How to Write a Novel*, Gordon states that:

James has practically obliterated himself as narrator. His stories are not told; they are acted out as if on a stage. He does not *tell* you anything about his characters; he lets them reveal themselves to you by what they say and do.

(1957: 124–5)

So, to return to two of our three central questions in this chapter: Did James develop a consistent theory of the point of view in narrative? Did he turn this into a rule?

HENRY JAMES AND POINT OF VIEW

The short answer to both questions is 'no'. But to answer our questions more fully, it is important that we examine exactly what James said, as distinct from what he has been conveniently reported as having said.

It is worth reminding ourselves here of one of James's key ways of thinking about novels, as discussed in Chapter 1. 'I cannot imagine', he wrote in 'The Art of Fiction', 'composition existing in a series of blocks': 'A novel is a living thing, all one and continuous, like any other organism, and in proportion as it lives will it be found, I think, that in each of the parts there is something of each of the other parts' (1884: 54). Whereas Trilling disliked formal neatness, James was addicted to it. 'Don't let anyone persuade you', James wrote to the novelist Hugh Walpole (1884–1941), 'that strenuous selection and comparison are not the very essence of art',

and that Form *is* [not] substance to that degree that there is absolutely no substance without it. Form alone *takes*, and holds and preserves, substance – saves it from the welter of helpless verbiage that we swim in as in a sea of tasteless tepid pudding.

(1912: 619)

Formless novels, for James, involve narrators, or narrator-agents, who survey all the characters and move in and out of their minds throughout the story. These novels lack what he calls in his preface to

Roderick Hudson a 'centre', or 'point of command' (1907–9: 1050). In his novel, *Roderick Hudson* (1875), Roderick is a young sculptor who travels to Italy with Rowland Mallett in a trip that Rowland arranges and finances. Instead of moving in and out of both characters, James restricts the point of view to Rowland. Furthermore, the novel is much less about what either character does, much more about how Rowland processes his experience of Roderick. 'From this centre the subject has been treated', James tells his reader, and 'from this centre the interest has spread' (1907–9: 1050).

Rowland, in Booth's terms, is the only narrator-agent. The novel is written in the third person, however, so that we can see Rowland as a disguised narrator whose consciousness is refracted through a pervasive outer narrator. Rowland's is the point of view, the angle of vision, but the voice is that of an undramatized third-person narrator. As we shall see in the next section, 'Consciousness', James constructed a wide variety of consciousnesses in his fiction and allocated a number of different roles to them. His distinctive contribution to narrative method is not just the development of restricted points of view, but the extent to which he made the consciousnesses of these

FOCALIZATION AND VOICE

The French narratologist Gérard Genette, whose work we shall discuss in 'After James, Trilling, and Booth', argued that the phrase 'point of view' conflated two elements that should be isolated for the purposes of analysis: 'focalization' (Genette 1980: 189) and 'voice' (1980: 213). The focalizer is rather like a camera-eye. That's the perspective from which we see the story. But we need to ask two questions: not just 'Who sees?' but 'Who speaks?' Focalizer and voice may well be different. In *Roderick Hudson*, the focalizer is Rowland Mallett for much of the time; but the voice is often that of the undramatized narrator. James was fully aware of the need for this kind of distinction even though he did not use these terms.

disguised narrators the main object of interest for the reader: '[t]he centre of interest throughout "Roderick" is in Rowland Mallett's consciousness, and the drama is the very drama of that consciousness' (1907–9: 1050).

Similarly, James specifies Christopher Newman as the centre of the novel in his preface to *The American* (1877): 'the thing constitutes itself organically as *his* adventure' (1907–9: 1067). It is made even clearer in that preface that this move helps James to avoid a dominating undramatized narrator (although there is one: like *Roderick Hudson*, this is not a first-person narrative) whose task is to offer an extensive narrative commentary. Newman is the one 'lighted figure', and we are seated by his side, looking at his view from the 'window'. We are restricted to '*his* vision, *his* conception, *his* interpretation' (1907–9: 1067–8). In the preface to *The Wings of the Dove*, centres of consciousness become 'vessel[s] of sensibility' (1907–9: 1292). As such, they are the means by which form and substance can be fused and an organic unity achieved. James does not restrict himself to one centre of consciousness, but uses 'successive centres' as 'happy points of view' (1907–9: 1294). The character, Kate Croy, is described as a 'reflector' (a word James often used for the centre of consciousness, along with 'register') who 'determine[s] and rule[s]'. There is no 'economy of treatment without an adopted, a related point of view'; and there can be 'no sacrifice of the recording consistency, that doesn't rather scatter and weaken' (1907–9: 1297). James's use of 'impersonal' is rather different from Booth's in this preface. For Booth, impersonal narration is the attempt to eliminate narrators; for James, who makes no distinction between authors and undramatized narrators, authorial intervention is impersonal because it detaches the reader from his centres of consciousness. The insertion of what he calls this 'impersonal plate' into the narrative is 'likely to affect us as an abuse of privilege' (1907–9: 1299). Does this mean, then, that James really did adhere to the kind of narrow thinking about point of view later ascribed to him, and that he sought relentlessly to eliminate narrative commentary? Not at all; as we shall find out, to begin with, by looking at his preface to *What Maisie Knew*.

One of James's boldest experiments with point of view is in *What Maisie Knew* (1897). The novel revolves around a young girl whose parents divorce. She is the innocent (although increasingly less so as she matures) means by which James registers the duplicity and immorality of her parents as they conduct a number of affairs for which they often use her as the conduit. The preface to *What Maisie Knew* shows that James was not only aware of Genette's distinction between focalization and voice, but also of the undesirability in this novel of giving both the angle of vision and the voice to Maisie. What James meant by point of view already looks rather less straightforward and simplistic than some of the later theorists have attributed to him.

For the first part of the novel, at least, James strives to 'register' the 'child's confused and obscure notation' in language deployed by the third-person narrative voice (1907–9: 1160). 'Maisie's terms accordingly play their part':

> but our own commentary constantly attends and amplifies. This it is that on occasion, doubtless, seems to represent us as going so 'behind' the facts of her spectacle as to exaggerate the activity of her relation to them.

James claims that it is 'her relation, her activity of spirit, that determines all our own concern – we simply take advantage of these things, better than she herself' (1907–9: 1161). It would be difficult to find a clearer account of what Genette means by focalization and voice. Maisie sees and the third-person undramatized narrator speaks. We are a long way here from Gordon's contention that James's 'stories are not told; they are acted out as if on a stage' (Gordon 1957: 124–5), and from the idea that he held to any rules (or required others to) when it came to point of view. James certainly stated that he had 'never . . . embraced the logic of any superior process' to that of having 'centres' (1907–9: 1297), but he had a much more flexible sense of what this amounted to than many of his subsequent critics.

This flexibility is clearly in evidence in his final essay on fiction, 'The New Novel' (James 1914). 'We take for granted', he wrote, 'a primary author', a concept related to Booth's implied author, 'take him so much for granted that we forget him in proportion as he works upon us, and that he works upon us most in fact by making us forget him' (1914: 275). Yet James goes on to express his admiration for the kind of conspicuous story-telling he found in Conrad's *Heart of Darkness*. In such novels there is 'a reciter, a definite responsible intervening first person singular' (1914: 275). Behind that narrator, James also identifies, however, 'the omniscience, remaining indeed nameless, though constantly active, which sets Marlow's omniscience in motion' (1914: 276). Conrad mobilizes both dramatized and undramatized narrators. Far from condemning the overt story-telling involved, James approves of the 'drama' between Marlow and this outer story-teller.

JAMES AND DRAMATIC NARRATIVE

James is nervous about going behind the facts of Maisie's spectacle in this novel (1907–9: 1161). But, in keeping with a commitment to the principle that subjects should determine their own treatment, he never turned any one way of writing a novel into a rule for all others. *The Awkward Age* (1899) is conceived in a sequence of sections that are like the 'successive Acts of a Play' (1907–9: 1131). What James seeks here is a form of 'objectivity' (1907–9: 1131) very different from the controlled subjectivity he can achieve through restricting the point of view to centres of consciousness. The subject of the novel is the irresponsible exposure of Nanda Brookenham (who is adolescent, or at an 'awkward age') to the immoral society occupied by her mother. The reader is presented with a number of 'aspects' of the subject, and the 'central object' is this 'situation' (1907–9: 1130). James does not go behind the characters here; but neither is his method that of the point of view. The novel has 'many distinct lamps'; and each of these lamps, or aspects, 'would be the light of a single "social occasion"' (1907–9: 1131).

One way of avoiding the 'perfect paradise of the loose end' (1907–9: 1134), which the English novel typified for James, was to restrict the point of view to a centre or centres of consciousness; but he envisaged and adopted a number of others. We have seen that the situation, rather than any one character, is the centre in *The Awkward Age*. For a while, James considered things (the property the characters fight over) as a centre in *The Spoils of Poynton* before settling on one of the characters (1907–9: 1144). Miriam Rooth, in *The Tragic Muse*, is the 'objective' (1907–9: 1112) centre but not the centre of consciousness. We hear what other characters say about her, and they all revolve around her central position in the novel. But we never know what she is thinking, only what some of the other characters think she is thinking.

It is not that James is being inconsistent here, or somehow unfaithful to a doctrine of the point of view he never espoused. Formal variety was a problem for his successors, but not for him. Booth argues relentlessly that no one method can be right, but that everything depends on the subject in hand. James agrees. He rejects *in this novel*

> that 'going behind', to compass explanations and amplifications, to drag out odds and ends from the 'mere' storyteller's great property-shop of aids to illusion.
>
> (1907–9: 1131)

But he insists that:

> 'Kinds' are the very life of literature ... I myself have scarcely to plead the cause of 'going behind', which is right and beautiful and fruitful in its place and order.
>
> (1907–9: 1131)

James borrowed another important device from the theatre to introduce variety into his narratives, and to avoid the possible suffocation of being restricted to one or two centres of consciousness. In first-person narratives, a character has to describe what he or she sees when looking into a mirror if we are to get a sense of her features. Alternatively, another character can say things such as 'I've always admired your beauty', and so on. James calls these characters 'ficelles'. They are a way of forwarding the narrative without having large chunks of undramatized narrative commentary. Ficelles are described by James

KINDS AND GENRE

'Genre' is another word for 'kinds'. When we talk about the genre of a novel (whether it is a novel of social realism, or a detective story, and so on), we are thinking about what 'kind' of novel it is. This takes us back to James's belief in 'The Art of Fiction' that kinds of novels are rather like organisms; and that these have, or should have, a form appropriate to their particularity.

FICELLES

'Ficelle' is a French word for a trick, or stage-device. James's ficelles, devices transposed into prose fiction from the theatre, are identical with Booth's disguised narrators. Their function is to take off the narrator's hands the work of supplying or eliciting information about characters and events.

as being 'but wheels to the coach'; they neither belong to 'the body of that vehicle (1907–9: 1161)', nor are they 'accommodated with a seat inside' (1907–9: 1082). There is a bit of a sleight-of-hand here. James can integrate the commentary of these characters into the novel, and preserve a sense of its formal unity, but their role as disguised narrative agents is close to that of the mere observers Booth identified, and they are often not far from being dramatized narrators. A represented ficelle, mediated by a third-person narrator, is not the same as a ficelle who walks on to the stage and speaks immediately. This is often overlooked by those who see James's novels as being like plays. Emphatically, then, James did not advocate the use of restricted points of view as the only narrative method. Neither did he turn this method into a rule for others.

CONSCIOUSNESS

I want briefly to introduce now, mostly as a way of preparing the ground for the final two chapters, some of the wider epistemological and moral issues relating to point of view and consciousness.

In his preface to *The Portrait of a Lady*, James gave an account of the relationship between consciousness and the novel that takes us some way from a narrow concern with narrative method. I want to quote this at length, not least because its language and ideas are central to the next, and especially to the last, chapter. It also helps us to see that James's preoccupation with points of view, centres of consciousness, and aspects does indeed reach out well beyond narratology.

> The house of fiction has in short not one window, but a million – a number of possible windows not to be reckoned, rather; every one of which has been pierced, or is still pierceable, in its vast front, by the need of the individual vision and by the pressure of the individual will. These apertures, of dissimilar shape and size, hang so, all together, over the human scene that we might have expected of them a greater sameness of report than we find. They are but windows at the best, mere holes in a dead wall, disconnected, perched aloft; they are not hinged doors opening straight upon life. But they have this mark of their own that at each of them stands a figure with a pair of eyes, or at least with a field-glass, which forms, again and again, for observation, a unique instrument, insuring to the person making use of it an impression distinct from every other. . . . [These] aperture[s] . . . are . . . as nothing without the posted presence of the watcher.
>
> (1907–9: 1075)

James adopts, where he does, a restricted point of view not just because of his passion for formal unity. He believes that the world, or an individual's experience of it, appears different according to who is looking and where he or she is standing. James saw this as the only

CONSCIOUSNESS

The word 'consciousness' derives from the Latin *conscius*: sharing knowledge with. Its moral dimension becomes clear once we realize that 'conscience', some kind of inner sense of what is right and wrong, has similar Latin roots. It comes from *conscientia*, which means 'knowledge' and 'awareness'. In keeping with these origins of the word 'consciousness', the 'moral consciousness' for James is a flexible and responsive awareness negotiated with others, maintained socially, and renovated by a mind, or intelligence, compelled to navigate complex experience.

morally healthy view; and this is the focus of Chapter 6, together with the often conflicting opinions on this issue held by Trilling and Booth. In this extract from the preface to *The Portrait of a Lady*, James's emphasis is on the boundless array of perspectives available to individuals, on the different impressions each person develops of his or her world, and on the degree to which how we look at the world is a way of shaping it.

What matters about points of view organized around centres of consciousness for James is the 'consciousness' as much as the centralizing. James's centres are described as having different degrees of awareness. He is anxious, going back to *Roderick Hudson*, that Rowland's consciousness should be 'sufficiently acute', but not too 'acute' (1907–9: 1050). Christopher Newman in *The American* has a 'wide', but only 'quite sufficiently wide, consciousness' (1907–9: 1067–8). James debates at length in his preface to *The Princess Casamassima* the 'danger of filling too full any supposed and above all any obviously limited vessel of consciousness' (1907–9: 1089); such centres must not be 'too *interpretative* of the muddle of fate' (1907–9: 1090). He wanted 'polished' mirrors (1907–9: 1095), 'intense *perceivers*' and 'ardent observer[s]' (1907–9: 1096), but he also limited the privilege of these centres. One reason for this is that as the nineteenth century wore on, as we saw at the outset of this chapter, critics, readers, and novelists alike had become impatient with omniscience. But then so had a number of scientists and philosophers. The old certainties were giving way to considerable uncertainty, and the relation between these new ways of thinking and James's narrative method is often overlooked.

James limits his consciousnesses in the interests of realism. But there are two dimensions to this realism. First of all, there was that growing suspicion of omniscience, and a corresponding condemnation in many quarters of all that 'going behind'. But, second, there was also an increasing interest in the idea that no experience of the world can be objective. As James said in his *Portrait of a Lady* preface, each 'impression' is 'distinct from every other' (1907–9: 1075). James is in the same groove here as the German philosopher Nietzsche (1844–1900): in 1887 Nietzsche declared in his 'On the Genealogy of Morals' that '[t]here is only seeing from a perspective, only a knowing from a perspective' (Nietzsche 1887: 153). In 'Why James, Trilling, and Booth', we mentioned the influence of 'pluralism' on Wayne C. Booth. Our concentration here is on Booth as a theorist of the novel, so a detailed

PLURALISM

In his 'Afterword' to the second edition of *The Rhetoric of Fiction*, Booth illustrates what he means by 'pluralism' like this: questions we choose to ask of, say, any novel 'work like our choices of optical instruments, each camera or microscope or telescope uncovering what other instruments conceal and obscuring what other instruments bring into focus' (1983a: 405). All views are valid; and all are partial.

consideration of his major work on pluralism — *Critical Understanding: The Powers and Limits of Pluralism* (1979) — is beyond the scope of this book. It is relevant to note, however, that Booth battles in *Critical Understanding* to fend off the idea that pluralism is the same thing as relativism or subjectivism. He believes in the need for, and existence of, different perspectives; and these correspond closely to the partial truths James saw each perceiver as possessing from his or her particular vantage-point. As the critic Susan Lanser reminds us, for Booth 'point of view concerns not simply the transmission of a story, but the communication of values and attitudes' (Lanser 1981: 45). Therefore, in keeping with the moral clarity he champions in *The Rhetoric of Fiction*, Booth is not prepared to accept a mere 'perspectivism'. He wrestles constantly with how all these perspectives might add up, with how they 'relate' and 'are to be assessed' (Booth 1979: 33).

For James, what we know is a function of how we look at our experience. He constructs limited centres of consciousness, not only as an acknowledgement of this reality, but as the very means of dramatizing the process. Form and content, or method and subject, become intertwined. Limited vision, and the consequences for characters who fail to recognize their limitations, is one of the great themes of James's novels. It is inseparable as a theme from the narrative methods he adopted, and from his theories of consciousness and experience. Our engagement in James's *The American*, for example, is not only with the tangle of the plot, but also with the tangled thinking of Newman as the centre of consciousness. We are pretty well restricted to Strether's 'sense of . . . things' in *The Ambassadors*; and his sense can only be incomplete. This is the point. The narrative method is a representation of how James believes consciousness works; and Strether's 'gropings'

(James 1907–9: 1313) in the world of experience are at the core of the novel's subject. The use and significance of such interpretative and moral gropings form a major part of our final two chapters.

SUMMARY

The main focus of this chapter has been on James's concepts of points of view and centres of consciousness. For some novels, James advocated restricting the angle of vision to one or two characters in order to reduce the amount of undramatized narration. These characters are not just camera-eyes, however; their consciousness, or limited awareness, of the world becomes part of both the method and subject. In this context, we also looked at James's anticipation of the two questions Genette thought we should ask when thinking about point of view – 'Who sees?' 'Who speaks?' – and at the related concepts of focalization and voice. We began by surveying some of Trilling's views. He was interested in the formal properties of texts, and in some aspects of narrative method; but he felt that an excessive concentration on form, a crime he saw the New Critics as committing, was detrimental to fiction. The world of experience is rough and full of loose-ends. Formally tight novels cannot adequately represent this for Trilling. We moved on to raise three central questions about James and point of view: Did James develop a consistent theory of the point of view in narrative? Did he turn this into a rule? Can it be detached from his wider epistemological and moral preoccupations? Some of the context of the reaction against omniscience in the later nineteenth century was discussed before we turned explicitly to these questions. The answers? James's views were inconsistent because he believed that the subject should determine the narrative method. He was broadly opposed to intrusive narration, to going behind, the characters; but he did not make a rule of this. We concluded, as a way of preparing for what follows, by looking at correspondences between James's narrative methods and an increasing interest, at a time when he was writing the prefaces and before, in consciousness and experience. James limited the perspectives from which his characters experience the world because he wanted to dramatize their 'gropings' as a way of representing the reality of the experiencing consciousness. His narrative methods, then, are inseparable from his wider epistemological and moral preoccupations.

5

READERS, READING, AND INTERPRETATION

All three of our theorists have a good deal to say about readers, reading, and interpretation. The purpose of this chapter is to compare and contrast the views of James, Trilling, and Booth on these issues in relation to aspects of the model of narrative communication on p. 16. I want to begin by suggesting how that model can be used to understand some of the principal ways of thinking about reading that have developed from around the later eighteenth century to the time of Trilling and Booth. By the end of the chapter, we shall be in a position to see where, and to what extent, our theorists fit into this scheme. Rather than considering each writer in turn, I want to look at their respective thinking on key, often overlapping elements, of the reading process. After two introductory sections, the sequence will be: types of reader; authors and readers; reading and autonomy; and the roles of the reader.

The texts under scrutiny here are James's 'The Art of Fiction' (1884) and his prefaces to the New York Edition (1907–9), Trilling's *The Liberal Imagination* (1950), *The Opposing Self* (1955b), and *Beyond Culture* (1965), and Booth's *The Rhetoric of Fiction* (1961), *Critical Understanding: The Powers and Limits of Pluralism* (1979), and *The Company We Keep: An Ethics of Fiction* (1988a). Booth's *The Company We Keep* will mostly be at the centre of the next chapter. *Critical Understanding* is preoccupied less with theories of the novel and more with criticism and critical thinking in general. For this reason, it has not figured to a large extent in this book. It does extend and revise, however, what *The Rhetoric of Fiction* has to say about reading.

MIMESIS AND EXPRESSION

The American critic M. H. Abrams, whose classic study is *The Mirror and the Lamp: Romantic Theory and the Critical Tradition* (1953), exerted a powerful influence on Wayne C. Booth. He is one of the critics considered at length in Booth's *Critical Understanding*. Richard Kearney summarizes Abrams' central argument in this way: 'The *mimetic* paradigm of imagining is replaced by the *productive* paradigm . . . the imagination ceases to function as a mirror reflecting some external reality and becomes a lamp which projects its own internally generated light onto things' (Kearney 1988: 155). This way of characterizing the Romantic imagination appeals to Booth because it corresponds with and reinforces his sense of the writing and reading of novels as acts of communication. An emphasis on a passive, mirror-like, reflection of reality (where the author's expression is an unnecessary intrusion at best) is succeeded by a re-orientation in which the author's expression, always rhetorical for Booth, becomes part of a 'conversation'. In this light, novels cease to be bounded objects such as mirrors in which there is a clear separation between the inside and the outside: 'suppose we abandon', Booth suggests, 'the metaphor of inside-versus-outside and view texts and their interpretations as a kind of conversation or dialogue between a text and a reader' (Booth 1979: 237). This takes us

THE MIRROR AND THE LAMP

Abrams chooses the metaphors of the mirror and the lamp for the writing process because he seeks to identify a shift that defines the difference between Romantic literature (a European-wide literary movement that stretched from the later eighteenth century through to the 1820s and 1830s) and what went before and came after. Until this period, Abrams believes, texts were seen as reflectors of the world (mirrors); from the time of Romanticism on, the emphasis was on production and the author's self-expression (lamps).

to a preliminary consideration of five models of the reading process that we shall ultimately use to describe the theories of reading held by James, Trilling, and Booth.

FIVE MODELS OF THE READING PROCESS

The shift in the Romantic period to seeing works of literary art as forms of self-expression, as productive rather than reflective of reality, posed some problems for the novel. As we saw in Chapter 2, the primary responsibility of the novelist has always been to forms of realism and representation (however these are defined). But for fiction to be regarded as an art form, there had to be an aesthetic distance between it and the author, reader, and text. It could be seen, for sure, as representing the world of everyday experience; but it must also be different from that world – not least in terms of its evident formal control and clear sense of composition – to be categorized as art. This requirement helps to explain the careful (and not always successful) balancing act in James between realism, the illusion of realism, and the formal demands of art. The theory of art as self-expression seemed appropriate for poetry: poets had the licence to create alternative, superior, realities, or to indulge in fantasy. These indulgences were much less available for a novelist such as James with his commitment to the 'air of reality' (James 1884: 53). Furthermore, the pressure to achieve objectivity, some kind of pure fiction, or an autonomous text, ran counter to this emphasis on self-expression. Tensions between the novel as a form of expression and as a self-contained work run throughout Booth's *The Rhetoric of Fiction*; they also inform our four models of the reading process.

The first model can be represented as follows:

1 **AUTHOR** → [TEXT] → READER

The Romantic emphasis on self-expression diverted the attention of critics and readers from the text's correspondences with the world and towards its relation to the author. The text (in square brackets to indicate this) was not just a work of art; principally, it was the vehicle for the author's expression of his unique personality, sensibility, and powers of imagination. The author is the most important element in this model. Texts were read to find out more about this distinctive, creative self; and they were often judged on the reader's estimations of his or her sincerity. Did the writer's life (and hence the increasing importance of biographical criticism), for instance, correspond with his expression of self in the text? This is a transmission model of reading in which the author and his intentions remain supreme and the reader is, more or less, a passive player in the game. Novels were read less as representations of the world, more for what they told you about the overall moral position of the author. Lacking, not even desiring, Booth's concept of the implied author, readers are happy in this model to conflate authors and narrators. Narrators express the author's views; and those views are an index of his moral and social integrity. This model of reading dominated the critical scene from the Romantic period through to the later decades of the nineteenth century. It remains as the popular, even intuitive, view of the reading process.

Our second and third models ran in parallel with the first; but it was possible to subscribe to the first without bothering much about the second and third. The difference between the second and third models is small but highly significant. Like the first, the second and third models are by no means defunct or useless for the modern critic:

> 2 SOCIETY ⟷ AUTHOR → TEXT → READER ⟷ SOCIETY

> 3 SOCIETY ⟷ AUTHOR → TEXT ⟷ READER ⟷ SOCIETY

In these models, the author loses his pre-eminence in that his society, and his interaction with that society, is taken into account. Not just their society, but history in general, has a formative impact on how and what he or she writes; and what is written, in turn, may affect society. The reader needs to know not just about the life of the author, but about his life and times. Fundamentally, however, this is still a transmission model. The reader might have a variety of things to do;

but he or she is still on the receiving end of the novel. In both the second and third models, there is some scope for looking at ways in which a particular reader's society shapes his or her expectations and reading competences. The fundamental difference between the second and third models is that in the third, the reader is seen as having an active role to play in reading and interpreting the text. James, Trilling, and Booth certainly see the reader as having plenty to do. But they differ enormously when it comes to the nature and extent of activity they see as possible or desirable.

The fourth model takes us firmly into the territory of New Criticism with its fervour for self-contained texts.

4   [AUTHOR] → **|| TEXT ||** → READER

The author, and of course his or her society or context, is practically irrelevant in this model. The text becomes, so to speak, a well-wrought urn (Brooks 1947): it is established as a palpable object sealed off from the taint of authorial expression, history, and the feelings of its readers. The reader's task is merely to contemplate, understand, and admire. We are a long way, in this model, from Booth's novel-as-conversation.

The final model is associated with what has become known as 'reader-response' theory.

5   [AUTHOR] → [TEXT] ← **READER**

Booth argues, reasonably enough, that such theories arose in part 'as a reaction against the heavy and uncritical emphasis' of the New Critics on the 'autonomous text' (1979: 255). Stanley Fish was one of the earliest American proponents of reader-response theory; but work on the reader's role in the construction of meaning had been going on for some time in Germany (see Iser 1974). Fish's essays on reading were first published in the 1970s before being revised and collected into a single volume (Fish 1980). The movement from model 1 to model 5, roughly from around 1780 or so to 1980, is the movement from a focus on the author and his life and times, through an addiction to textual autonomy, to a (counter-intuitive) emphasis on the reader as the writer of the text. In just over two hundred years, the reader was transformed from being the passive receiver of a text embodying the author's intentions into having such an active role in construction and interpretation that he or she became, effectively or actually, the writer of the text. (The square brackets indicate how tenuous and contingent the positions of both author and text have become.) The French theorist Roland Barthes (1915–80) crystallizes this transformation: there is one place where the 'multiplicity' of the 'text' is 'focused and that place is the reader, not, as was hitherto said, the author . . . a text's unity lies not in its origin but in its destination' (Barthes 1968: 1469).

By the end of this chapter, then, we shall be in a position to situate James, Trilling, and Booth in relation to these models. I shall refer to them, in fact, throughout our discussion.

TYPES OF READER

All models, of course, simplify; and they often overlap. James divided readers into four categories that sprawl across our five models: the uncritical reader at large; the professional critic, or reviewer; the intelligent, sophisticated, experienced reader; and Henry James.

In 'The Art of Fiction', James characterizes both the reader at large and the professional critic, until the advent of the kind of theoretical self-consciousness he associates with the French, as being capable of no more than the simplest pleasures of merely passive and self-indulgent consumption:

> During the period I have alluded to there was a comfortable, good-humoured feeling abroad that a novel is a novel, as a pudding is a pudding, and that our only business with it could be to swallow it. But within a year or two . . . there have been signs of returning animation.
>
> (James 1884: 44)

But other readers, clearly of the 'intelligent' variety, can appreciate the 'form . . . after the fact' and 'enjoy one of the most charming of pleasures': that of judging the extent to which the potential of the subject has been realized (1884: 50). Subsequent commentators have made bold assertions about how keen James was to involve readers in the business of creative reading and imaginative interpretation (Pearson 1997). To a degree, this is true. But he was nervous about the interference of even his most intelligent readers. In any event, as we can see from surveying the prefaces, James continued to hold a highly stratified sense of his readership, and was often contemptuous of readers in general.

The form of the novel, how it is 'done', was one of its main interests for James; and he was intolerant of, and derogatory towards, readers at large and critics who failed to share this enthusiasm. For the purpose of detecting this 'interest', he characteristically observes, 'even the reader will do, on occasion' (1907–9: 1044). But for such 'intimate appreciations . . . ninety-nine readers in a hundred have no use whatever' (1907–9: 1062). He longed for some 'Paradise . . . where the direct appeal to the intelligence might be legalised' (1907–9: 1082); but he is forced to concede that 'the reader with the idea or the suspicion of a structural centre is the rarest of friends and of critics' (1907–9: 1108). He does write of 'wary reader[s]' (1907–9: 1090), 'fellow witnesses' (1907–9: 1160), and the 'cunning reader' (1907–9: 1256); more frequently, however, he continues to rail against the 'broad-backed public' (1907–9: 1233) and to condemn their 'grossness' (1907–9: 1271). In his essay, 'The Future of the Novel', James describes the 'immense public' as 'inarticulate, but abysmally absorbent' (1899: 100). In the main, they are 'constituted by boys and girls' (and by the latter, James also means unmarried women) (1899: 100–1). These are among the 'millions for whom taste is but an obscure, confused, immediate instinct' (1899: 101). These are the indiscriminating omnivores of 'The Art of Fiction'. There are also 'indifferent' readers who have never set much store by the novel; and there are those who have become 'alienated' because of the proliferation of novels at the end of the nineteenth century (1899: 101).

James regarded writers, especially himself, as the best readers, not least because he felt that successful reading depended on being able to detect the original intentions of the writer by inferring what his initial subject was and then applying the 'test of execution' (1884: 50). 'I re-write you, much, as I read', he told the English novelist H. G. Wells (1866–1946), 'which is the highest tribute my damned impertinence can pay an author' (1900: 132–3). Two comments help us to see that the prefaces represented for James a privileged, and incomparable, reading of his own fiction, and the extent to which he was prepared to shut out incompetent readers and critics. To William James in 1890 he wrote that 'one has always a "public" enough if one has an audible vibration – even if it should only come from one's self' (1890b: 300). James saw this reader, himself, as conterminous with the author; and it is clear that model 5 would be a good fit for him: '[t]he teller of a story is primarily . . . the listener to it, the reader of it too' (1907–9: 1089). As for professional critics, or reviewers, James subordinates them to a highly passive role. He sees them at best as mediators for readers at large. They can be, but rarely are, 'the real helper of the artist, a torch-bearing outrider, the interpreter, the brother' (1891: 98). The critic is consigned to a 'vicarious' life as he merely translates, or explains, texts to other readers (1891: 99).

Trilling and Booth consider readers much more in the lump than does James. Trilling separates readers into only three broad formations: students, academic critics, and the more or less educated reader not involved in the academy. In the main, especially in *Beyond Culture*, he regards students and academic critics alike as docile domesticators of novels originally designed to stir the reader into life and action. This is certainly the upshot of what Booth describes as 'one of the best' essays Trilling wrote (Booth 1988a: 53n), 'On the Teaching of Modern Literature' (Trilling 1965: 3–27). Elsewhere in *Beyond Culture*, Trilling berates New Critical academics for instructing us in an 'intelligent passivity before the beneficent aggression' of the text: such criticism has 'taught us how to read certain books; it has not taught us how to engage them' (1965: 200). Throughout his writing, Trilling is much happier dealing with the fairly well-educated, middle-class reader at large. But he has a hopelessly homogeneous sense of this group. He described these 'educated' readers, who were often his main target, as 'people who value their ability to live some part of their lives with serious ideas' (1950: 89). Trilling's preface to *Beyond Culture*, in defending his use of 'we' to represent a 'natural continuity' of cultural values and responsiveness between disparate groups, concedes that his move was towards a totalized sense of readers and reading.

Booth has little time for discriminating between different groups of reader, although he is of course aware that some readers are better at it than others. Booth's reader has to be a kind of generalized 'everyman' (or 'woman') because he is committed to the idea that communication is a universal process that cuts across social, ethnic, and religious boundaries. Booth's adherence is always to what he calls 'common-sense attitude[s]' (1961: 105), and this sometimes makes him hostile (like Trilling) to theoreticians and academic critics. His main distinction, as we shall see later on in this chapter and in the next, is between successful and unsuccessful reading, and between reading that merely surrenders to the text and reading that challenges it in justifiable ways. Readers are much more important for Booth than they are for James because, like Aristotle, he sees the production of 'effects on audiences' as the purpose of art (Booth 1961: 92).

Since at least the appearance of Wolfgang Iser's *The Implied Reader* (published in 1972 and translated into English from the German in 1974), the concept of the 'implied reader' has been in circulation. Booth uses this phrase frequently in *Critical Understanding*; but in *The Rhetoric of Fiction* he writes about the 'postulated reader' (1961: 177). A discussion of the 'implied reader', however, should really be part of our next section.

AUTHORS AND READERS

This section is concerned with how James, Trilling, and Booth consider the relation between authors and readers in quite a specific sense. It necessarily overlaps with the next section, on 'autonomy', and a final section on 'functions'.

In an early essay entitled 'The Novels of George Eliot' (1866a), James anticipated one of Booth's most important concepts: the 'postulated', or 'implied', reader mentioned at the end of the last section. In this essay at least, James seems to be veering towards model 3 of the reading process; although we shall have to suspend judgement about that until the final section:

> In every novel the work is divided between the writer and the reader; but the writer makes the reader very much as he makes his characters. When he makes him ill, that is, makes him indifferent, he does no work; the writer does all. When he makes him well, that is, makes him interested, then the reader does quite half the labor.

Left to deduce some things for himself, the 'reader would be doing but his share of the task' (1866b: 922).

POSTULATED, MOCK, AND IMPLIED READERS

In *The Rhetoric of Fiction*, Booth writes approvingly of Walker Gibson's (1950) coinage of the phrase 'mock readers' (Booth 1961: 138), and he goes on to develop his own 'postulated reader'. Booth argues that the implied author (again, not just the narrator, if any, but the sum of all a text's elements) shapes readers who will go along with the novel and its system of values for at least some of the time.

Hence, the idea that a text makes its readers was not new when Gibson, Booth, and Iser embraced it with enthusiasm. But Booth, for one, extends the phrase by linking it to his concept of the implied author, and by establishing an unambiguously moral and ideological agenda for the reader-manufacturing author:

> It is not, after all, only an image of himself that the author creates. Every stroke implying his second self will help to mold the reader into the kind of person suited to appreciate such a character and the book he is writing.
>
> (1961: 89)

From the outset, Booth was interested in the power (or lack of it) the reader might, and should, have to resist this implied self.

Whereas James believes that giving novels neat, happy endings, and resolving all the problems makes the reader passive, his main concern is with the general artlessness of such fiction. Booth's preoccupation with the implied reader is, as ever, moral in that he is concerned about novels that might be willing and able to force their suspect values on weak readers. Trilling, however, anticipates much more clearly a reader-response approach to the role of the reader. It is less that he sees novels as making readers, more that he wants to emphasize an active, interpretative, role for them that is at once desirable and unavoidable. No reader, for Trilling, can ever be simply a passive consumer because this is to falsify the way that language works when it comes to the transmission of ideas. In the spirit of model 5, Trilling writes that:

> Too often we conceive of an idea as being like the baton that is handed from
> runner to runner in a relay race. But an idea as a transmissible thing is rather
> like the sentence that in the parlor game is whispered about in a circle; the
> point of the game is the amusement that comes when the last version is
> compared with the original.

(1950: 181)

But if texts survive, in part, by making or implying readers, and on the vitality of the interpretative whispering that goes on about them in the name of reading and criticism, where does that leave the autonomy trumpeted by the New Critics?

READING AND AUTONOMY

James's commitment to the organic unity of the text has been evident throughout this book; and there is an extent to which this suggests that novels have a vitality, a self-containment, or an essential independence from authors and readers. Yet the prefaces can be seen as an act of repossession in which James reanimates, or revitalizes, his texts by uniting them with germinating ideas, or subjects, that have largely been lost on the readers of his fiction. On the one hand, James offers his novels as rounded works of art that are reader-proof; on the other, he everywhere implies that they are lifeless unless readers can apply that 'test of execution' by detecting the original conception of each novel's subject.

The prefaces supplement the novels; this means that they are very far from the autonomous artefacts the New Critics wanted to take them for. This revitalizing process is not always possible, however, for in some novels 'the buried secrets, the intentions, are buried too deep to rise again' (1907–9: 1046). You will recall that the New Critics secured the autonomy of the text by detaching it from the author's intentions and the reader's feelings. But James was a full-blooded intentionalist, as was Booth. Nearly a decade before 'The Art of Fiction', James wrote that a novel is more likely to hang 'well together . . . when there has been a definite intention – that intention of which artists who cultivate "art for art" are usually so extremely mistrustful' (1876: 170). Given that, on the whole, James believes that his readers are generally unable to identify such intentions, he offers some in his prefaces.

For Booth, as for James, 'it is only when texts are torn free of intentions that they become uninterpretable' (Booth 1979: 265). Similarly, Trilling had no patience with any fear that the reader might compromise an illusory (and impossible) textual autonomy by making 'reference to something beyond the work itself' (Trilling 1950: 271). He also felt that to insist on textual autonomy was to interfere 'with our private and personal relation to the literary work', and to prevent 'our freedom to respond to it in our own way' (Trilling 1965: 163). Trilling and Booth are as explicitly opposed to the 'affective' and 'intentional' fallacies as James is implicitly so.

THE ROLE OF THE READER

We are now in a position to make a clearer assessment of where James, Trilling, and Booth stand in relation to our five models of the reading process. We shall make it by looking at how each sees the roles, tasks, or functions of the reader.

For James, then, the main function of the reader (his 'intelligent' reader) is to identify the subject of the novel as it first arose in the writer's imagination and then to try to judge the degree to which it has been successfully developed. Among the questions James asks as a reader, and expects his readers to be able (ideally) to ask are: Does the overall treatment of the subject seem appropriate? Subjects imply purposes. Are these purposes closely related to what emerge, on reading the novel, as the author's intentions? Does the novel, for example, have a formal unity in terms of a recognizable centre, or a suitably polished centre or centres of consciousness?

The author turns his subject into an interesting novel by appreciating it (see p. 43). This process of appreciation is also an act of appropriation: the subject (which may originally have been an anecdote recounted to him, a dimension of his own experience, or whatever) becomes his. Reading is akin to writing because critical (careful, responsive) reading also involves appreciation and appropriation. James's readings and revisions of his novels are described as '*act[s] of re-appropriation*' (1907–9: 1330), and this is exactly how he characterizes reading at its best; as embodied, perhaps, only in himself: 'To criticise is to appreciate, to appropriate, to take intellectual possession, to establish in fine a relation with the criticised thing and make it one's own' (1907–9: 1169).

Again, James expects his rarefied reader to be analytical; but what he means by analysis is 'appreciation' and not interpretation as we might think of it: speculations about what the novel means, what its broader significance might be, and the like. For critical readers, especially in a university environment, reading usually amounts to going beyond the literal meaning of the text. This is rarely, if ever, what James means by reading. James's most celebrated story about reading and interpretation is 'The Figure in the Carpet' (1896). But the task of interpretation that defies its characters is the identification of the intentions of the author (Hugh Vereker) in the story, and not the pursuit of the wider meaning of his texts.

For Trilling (especially in *The Liberal Imagination* and *Beyond Culture*) there are three important and inseparable tasks for the reader: to assess how much damage a novel can do; to preserve its rough grain, rather than to use a New Critical plane to achieve a useless smoothness; and to bring to bear on any novel its social and historical context as a way of inspecting the moral health of the reader's self and society. For the New Critic engaged in 'close reading' (Trilling 1965: 161), texts are 'structures of words' (1965: 11) whose apparent contradictions, ambiguities, and ironies can always be read into coherence. But for Trilling, 'novelists as a class have made the most aggressive assault upon the world'; and novel readers, critics, and teachers should work hard to preserve 'the roughness of grain of the novel' (1950: 261). Novels do not transmit ideas as 'pellets of intellection' but as 'living things' (1950: 284). Where the critic comes up with a neat interpretation that irons out all the wrinkles, he has failed to realize that vital ideas are 'inescapably connected with our wills and desires', and 'susceptible of growth and development' (1950: 284). Ultimately, to see reading as an exercise in detecting or imposing formal unity is to reduce novels to objects of mere 'contemplation' (1950: 271). Novels are more like tanks than pyramids, and we should never tire of asking 'how much *damage*' they 'can do' (1965: 11) and what the benefit of that damage might be to the reader and society.

Trilling cannot accept that reading and interpretation require the detachment of novels from their historical context. His best account of this is in the section of *The Liberal Imagination* entitled 'The Sense of the Past'. Readers cultivate a 'historical sense', which involves realizing the extent to which we shape the past for our own purposes, so that they can connect the novel and its historical conditions with their reading of it. Trilling brought biography, the political context, and psychoanalysis, as well as a sense of history, to bear on his reading of the novel. He expected readers and critics at large to do the same.

Throughout *The Rhetoric of Fiction*, Booth is anxious to challenge what he sees as the futile pursuit of pure fiction with its dependence on the contrast between what is intrinsic and extrinsic to the text. He continues this challenge in *Critical Understanding* in an even more radical way:

> Suppose we abandon the metaphor of inside-versus-outside and view texts and their interpretations as a kind of conversation or dialogue between a text and a reader; this supposes a text that exists, when interpreted, at least as much *in* the reader and the reader's culture as *in* the author and the author's culture, and it also supposes a reader who, as he interprets, is at least as much *in* the text and in the author's culture as *in* his own culture.
>
> (Booth 1979: 237)

Successful conversations depend, for Booth, on the listener's being able to inhabit the world of the other person's mind. He believes that reading is a similar business. In fact, where the reader surrenders to

NARRATIVE AUDIENCE AND AUTHORIAL AUDIENCE

The 'narrative audience' is the credulous, all-believing, reader who accepts both the 'nonce beliefs' of the text (those that we might only hold while we are reading it) and its 'fixed norms' (beliefs on which the narrative depends which also operate in the real world of the reader). The 'authorial audience' accepts the 'nonce beliefs' only for the duration of the story and may or may not eventually reject the 'fixed norms'. Booth's example is the story of Mother Goose. The narrative audience believes that the story actually happened and has no doubt that geese can lay golden eggs. The authorial audience goes along with all this only when reading the story and is left wondering about whether he or she accepts a 'fixed norm' to do with greed in general, or whatever, that the story seems to be dramatizing (1988a: 142–8).

UNDERSTANDING AND OVERSTANDING

Booth defines 'understanding' as the 'process' of 'entering another mind' (1979: 262). Novels offer readers through their implied authors various values, moral attitudes, and so on; arguing with these, even repudiating them, and coming up with different perspectives on the world of the novel is what Booth means by 'overstanding'. 'Understanding', then, is the reader's reconstruction of what the text demands; when the reader recognizes the point at which the 'violation of its demands will prove necessary', he begins to 'overstand' (1979: 242).

the implied author of a novel, he occupies both the implied author's culture and that of his own; and the boundaries between implied author, text, and reader collapse.

'[T]he most successful reading', argues Booth in *The Rhetoric of Fiction*, 'is one in which the created selves' of implied author and implied reader 'can find complete agreement', and where the flesh-and-blood reader 'subordinate[s]' her 'mind and heart to the book' (1961: 138). Booth adopts a distinction in *The Company We Keep* first made by Peter Rabinowitz (1977) between the 'narrative audience' and the 'authorial audience'. The 'authorial audience', the 'implied author's mate' (Booth 1988a: 143n), is equivalent to the 'implied reader' and the 'flesh-and-blood reader' when the three are in harmony (see the model on p. 16). But this harmony is far from the end of the transaction for Booth. The flesh-and-blood reader can reject the implied reader of the novel in *The Rhetoric of Fiction*. In *Critical Understanding*, there is a duty to do so.

The role of the reader in *Critical Understanding* is first of all to 'understand' the text and then to 'overstand' it. Booth is close here to the ideas of E. D. Hirsch as they first appeared in 1960 (they were further developed, in 1967, in his *Validity in Interpretation*). Hirsch distinguishes between 'interpretation', or 'understanding', and 'criticism': 'interpretation' is the act of trying to retrieve the original intentions of the author, whereas criticism is more the attempt of a reader to understand the text on her own terms. Similarly, each novel, for Booth, sets its own *'boundaries* of "appropriateness"' (1979: 241), or the questions that can be asked.

In *The Company We Keep*, Booth identifies

> three kinds of question: those that the object seems to *invite* me to ask; those
> that it will *tolerate* or respond to, even though perhaps reluctantly; and those
> that *violate* its own interests or effort to be a given kind of thing in the world.
>
> (1988a: 90)

Overstanding begins when the reader imposes his own questions on (or violates) the text. Jane Austen's *Mansfield Park*, for example, raises questions about whether the impersonations necessary to acting in the amateur theatricals of the novel spill over into the insincerity of some of its characters. The critic Edward Said (1993), among others, has gone on to 'overstand' the text by concentrating rather more on why the slavery plantation on which the wealth of the Bertram family depends is ignored in the novel. Clearly, Jane Austen had no intention of dwelling on slavery. For Booth that's the point: overstanding, by raising a question the novel avoids, is a justifiable violation of the implied author's intentions. '[H]ow long we shall choose to remain engaged in the act of respectful understanding', Booth contends, 'will depend . . . on what the text has to say about its own value[s]' (1979: 335). '[T]he effort to understand', which is where the reader should always begin, 'is never the only proper goal of the critical path'. Once we have understood, there is no limit to the 'paths of overstanding' (1979: 335).

Where, then, does this leave James, Trilling, and Booth in relation to our five models of the reading process? There are elements of models 1 and 3 in James's approach; but he is often closer to the first model than the third. The author and his intentions are paramount in the prefaces; and the task of the reader established there is often merely that of trying to fathom out the relation between the two. Even where James wants the creative involvement of the reader (model 3), he limits his role to that of inferring the original plan, the initiating subject; what matters above all is the extent to which readers are able to admire James's compositional powers. Model 3 seems to suit Trilling well. He insists on the importance of the author's views and the society and history that frame them; but he also wants readers to engage with novels rather than simply to receive them passively. Booth would reject model 5 outright; and he would regard the others as vast simplifications of what successful novels should involve. We need a model 6 for Booth's sense of the reading process.

```
| IMPLIED AUTHOR → TEXT → IMPLIED READER |←→ READER AS
                                            AUTHORIAL
                                            AUDIENCE
                                         |←→ READER AS
                                            NARRATIVE
                                            AUDIENCE
```

The reader's first task is to understand the implied author by surrendering to his views and merging himself with the implied reader; the second task is to 'overstand' by going beyond the questions to which the text has sought to limit the implied reader. This inevitably involves the repudiation of the implied reader.

SUMMARY

We began by considering the shift from art as imitation, or mimesis, to art as expression in Romantic thinking. We were able to see how and in what ways the author was regarded as the most important element in the reading process for much of the nineteenth century. Our five models of the reading process, ultimately six, allowed us to trace the extent to which in approximately two hundred years (from 1780 to 1980, or thereabouts) the reader became the most dominant element. It was never going to be easy to apply these models of reading to James, Trilling, and Booth. For a start, they have very different views on how to characterize the range of available readers. Trilling and Booth have much more faith in some kind of 'universal reader' than James; and James oscillates between making impossible demands on his readers and holding them in contempt. When it comes to the relation between authors and readers, James anticipates the concept of the implied reader in that he sees the novel as making readers, the few he sees as responsive and intelligent, in the same way that it makes characters. But James wants his readers, in the main, to be dutiful; whereas Booth believes that they should be free to cast off the character imposed on them by the novel. To a degree, Trilling looks ahead to the much more active and creative role established for the reader by critics such as Stanley Fish. Neither Booth nor Trilling has any time for the textual autonomy insisted on by the New Critics, but for different reasons. For Booth, the novel is a conversation; and this means that the boundaries between text and reader are often arbitrary. Trilling thinks that screening out society and history makes novels powerless and readers passive. The main role of the reader, for James, is to admire his compositional skills by working out the original intention and gauging the success or otherwise of its execution. Trilling wants readers to be active engagers of the text and to appreciate novels as aggressive and oppositional when it comes to the dominant culture. Understanding, by which he means surrendering for a time to the implied reader, is the door to enjoyment and productive criticism for Booth. After that, the reader must overstand by rejecting the implied reader and asking questions the text has forbidden.

6

MORAL
INTELLIGENCE

It will be abundantly evident by now that questions of morality, however defined, are at the centre of the theory and criticism of James, Trilling, and Booth. The aim of this chapter is to examine in detail the attitudes towards morality and the novel of these three writers. It will also act as a consolidation of much of the argument that has gone before.

JAMES AND MORAL CONSCIOUSNESS

In a letter written as early as 1867, James argued that the American literature of the future would be characterized by its 'moral consciousness', its 'unprecedented spiritual lightness and vigour' (1867: 17). Consciousness, as we discovered in Chapter 4, is vital to James's theory of the novel. 'The Art of Fiction', to recapitulate some of what was discussed in Chapter 1, argues against the critic Walter Besant's view that the novel should have a 'conscious moral purpose' (James 1884: 62). For James, neither moral thinking nor the art of the novel should operate according to pre-determined rules. James distinguishes between formal matters, or 'questions of execution', and 'questions of morality' (narrowly defined). He sees the latter – particularly given the squeamishness towards sex, adultery, and immorality it encourages – as stifling fiction. If moral thinking is essential to James's theory of the novel, what does he mean in this context by 'moral?'

THE MORAL SENSE AND THE ARTISTIC SENSE IN 'THE ART OF FICTION'

James writes in 'The Art of Fiction' that:

> There is one point at which the moral sense and the artistic sense lie very near together; that is in the light of the very obvious truth that the deepest quality of a work of art will always be the quality of the mind of the producer . . . No good novel will ever proceed from a superficial mind.
>
> (1884: 63–4)

A similar idea is expressed in the preface to *The Portrait of a Lady*. The '"moral" sense of a work of art' depends 'on the amount of felt life concerned in producing it': 'The question comes back thus, obviously, to the kind and degree of the artist's prime sensibility, which is the soil out of which his subject springs'. 'Sense', especially the peculiarly intense sense of the highly intelligent novelist, connects the moral and the aesthetic for James. This is part of a long tradition of thinking that goes all the way back to the Greek philosopher Plato and beyond. One of its most well-known manifestations is in Keats's 'Ode on a Grecian Urn': 'Beauty is Truth, – Truth Beauty, – that is all / Ye know on earth, and all ye need to know' (1820: 321). Experience is at the core of the moral and the aesthetic. The moral and the artistic senses converge if we become 'one on whom nothing is lost' (James 1884: 53) as we encounter complex, ambiguous experiences.

We start to become moral, as James defines the word, only as we begin to realize that our perspective is partial and needs to take account of the perspectives of others. Art and morality are social affairs. Novelists and readers, like James's characters, need to develop their

SENSE

The 'sense' is a faculty of physical perception and experience. There are five principal senses: sight, hearing, smell, taste, and touch. For James, morality and art are both ways of experiencing the world and the results of such experience in the form of a heightened consciousness and a more acute imagination.

moral intelligence as they steep themselves in the complexity of experiencing the world. But as we saw in Chapter 1, for James 'experience is never limited and is never complete'. What matters is the extent to which 'The Art of Fiction' unites the experiencing subject with experience by suggesting that an 'immense sensibility' is the 'very atmosphere' of the 'mind' (James 1884: 52). Sensibility is always transitive; to be sensible, ultimately, is to be sensible of the world of experience. At this point, as a way of grasping just how inseparable art and morality are for James, you might find it helpful to review the discussion of perspective and consciousness in Chapter 4 (pp. 82–6).

Quite simply, James believes that to become an intelligent novelist is to reach a moral stature beyond narrow, conventional, thinking. He further believes that this should be a general aspiration, while still holding to the view that intelligence is often the preserve of the few. In such a world, he observes wistfully, 'are we not moreover – and let it pass this time as a happy hope! – pretty well all novelists now?' (1902a: 346). The novel, for both the writer and the reader, is the road not to moral principles, but to the moral sense; and where the novelist is intelligent, the novel will offer an experience that has the potential for shaping and developing the reader's own intelligence. The novel is 'the great extension, great beyond all others, of experience and of consciousness' (1907–9: 1061); and 'experience' is, for James, 'our appreciation and our measure of what happens to us as social creatures' (1907–9: 1091). If the novel is intelligently controlled, all the necessary moral ground will be covered, and 'all prate of its representative character, its meaning and its bearing, its morality and humanity, [is] an impudent thing' (1907–9: 1068). Novels should not transmit moral principles and rules as such, but renovate and develop the mind by attempting to engage the reader in the pursuit of intricate combinations of form, content, and germinating subjects.

James connects morality and realism in 'The Art of Fiction' by arguing that novelists should not limit what they represent to the morally exemplary by excluding aspects of human experience: 'the essence of moral energy is to survey the whole field' (1884: 63). Two things will guarantee the broader moral reach of the novel: the acuity of the novelist, and the degree to which his or her novels can stimulate critical investigation and reflection. James strikingly defined 'moral consciousness' as 'stirred intelligence' (1907–9: 1095) in his New York prefaces; and he believed that a sharp, responsive intellect and a sense of morality were much the same thing. The clarifying expression of some of these ideas came eight years before 'The Art of Fiction' in an essay entitled 'The Minor French Novelists' (1876):

> Every out-and-out realist *who provokes curious meditation* may claim that he is a moralist, for that, after all, is the most that the moralists can do for us. They sow the seeds of virtue; they can hardly pretend to raise the crop.
>
> (1876: 169–70, my emphasis)

TRILLING AND THE 'MORAL OBLIGATION TO BE INTELLIGENT'

In a 1971 talk at Purdue University, Trilling reflected on his experience as a student at Columbia College in the 1920s:

> The great word in the college was INTELLIGENCE. An eminent teacher of ours, John Erskine, provided a kind of slogan by the title he gave to an essay of his which, chiefly through its title, gained a kind of fame: THE MORAL OBLIGATION TO BE INTELLIGENT.
>
> (Wieseltier 2000: ix)

Intelligence, variably defined, is as important for Trilling as it is for James, and as inseparable from moral thinking and behaviour. Trilling, again like James, held that the novel is one of intelligence's most fearless allies. The novel at its best represented to him 'variousness and possibility, which implies the awareness of complexity and difficulty' (Trilling 1950: vi). It involves the reader 'in the moral life, inviting him to put his own motives under examination, suggesting that reality is not as his conventional education has led him to see it' (1950: 209).

Art and morality 'lie very near together' for James (1884: 63), but art embraces and subsumes morality. Similarly, in *Beyond Culture*, Trilling endorses Nietzsche's contention that 'art and not ethics constitutes the essential metaphysical activity of man' (Trilling 1965: 19–20). Like the German philosopher Hegel (1770–1831), and in line with aspects of James's 'The Art of Fiction', Trilling takes the view in *The Opposing Self* that 'the aesthetic is the criterion of the moral' (1955b: iv): it is the novel, through its formal complexity and superfine responsiveness to experience, that calls the moral to account (and not the other way round). Trilling's emphasis is less social than James's, however. His commitment is to the 'high authority of the self in its quarrel with culture and society' (1965: 89).

It is not just that conventional, rule-bound, morality opposes the self, but that it is distorted and compromised by society and culture. A question arises as to how Trilling reconciles what he sees as an antagonism between the most valuable novels and society, and his avowal of the 'classic defence of literary studies' in the late nineteenth century as the means by which 'an improvement in the intelligence' could be achieved; especially 'the intelligence as it touches the moral life' (Trilling 1965: 184). The answer to this question is in Trilling's view that this 'defence . . . supposed that literature carried the self beyond culture' (1965: 201), and that its function was to be 'subversive' (1965: 89). This brings us to one of Trilling's most important concepts: 'moral realism'.

MORAL REALISM

The phrase 'moral realism' was first used by Trilling in his 1943 study of the English novelist, E. M. Forster. Trilling owed some of his thinking about the novel and morality to Forster's views on the relation between fiction and society. James called *The Ambassadors* a 'drama of discrimination' and suggested that his character's 'gropings would figure among his most interesting motions' (James 1907–9: 1312–13). Trilling saw Forster as part of the same tradition, one emphasizing the importance of the individual's own negotiations with and navigations of social and moral thinking. He also, thinking back to our opening

MORAL REALISM

Rule-bound moral thinking usually operates on the basis of a simple distinction between what is right and wrong, or good and bad; and these terms, in turn, are often defined rigidly and simplistically. There are two ways in which Trilling's concept of 'moral realism' challenges much conventional moral thinking: first, the good and the bad, he believes, can hardly ever be neatly disentangled; second, morality requires constant 'discriminations and modifications' (1950: 82).

discussion in this chapter of James and 'moral consciousness', thought of it as a distinctively American tradition; and one initiated, in part, by Nathaniel Hawthorne.

'Moral realism' is 'not the awareness of morality itself but of the contradictions, paradoxes and dangers of living the moral life' (Trilling 1943b: 11–12). It is not the knowledge of 'good and evil, but the knowledge of good-and-evil' (1943b: 14). To see 'good and evil' as a binary opposition is to 'play the old intellectual game of antagonistic principles' (1943b: 15). To overcome this binary way of thinking, one Trilling associated with Marxism, imagination is necessary. Only in art, and especially in the novel, are paradox, complexity, and ambiguity welcome constituents. 'Forster refuses to be conclusive' (1943b: 16) about morality; he proposes that ideas 'are for his service and not for his worship' (1943b: 23).

TRILLING'S *SINCERITY AND AUTHENTICITY*

Much of Trilling's thinking about morality and the novel culminates in his last book (published in 1972), *Sincerity and Authenticity*. Its focus throughout is on the 'ceaseless flux' of the 'moral life' and on the extent to which 'the values . . . of one epoch are not those of another' (1972: 1). In line with the ideas of Rousseau, especially in his *Discourse on the Origin of Inequality* (1754), to live in society at all is inevitably to become corrupted. Conventional moral thinking, far from acting as a therapy in this regard, is merely a part of the raging disease: 'the moral judgement is not ultimate' (Trilling 1972: 32).

Trilling constructs his investigation of sincerity and authenticity around several key thinkers and novelists: among them are the French writer and philosopher Denis Diderot (1713–84), Rousseau, Nietzsche, and Freud. Diderot's *Rameau's Nephew* (written between 1761 and 1772, and published for the first time in 1805) is seen as an early demonstration of the way in which sincerity, the perform-ance of the self as a personality, stands in the way of that disintegration necessary to true selfhood. Later, not least because it registers how ambivalent a process this can be, Trilling takes Kurtz in Conrad's *Heart of Darkness* to be an example of self-disintegration as a form of social critique. Rousseau is a pivotal figure in the movement from sin-cerity to authenticity Trilling attempts to trace because he condemned

SINCERITY AND AUTHENTICITY

'Sincerity' was a particularly powerful social concept at the turn of the eighteenth century. Trilling sees it as the performance of a personality – the adoption of a guise of honesty, trustworthiness, and so on – with self-advantage as the goal. 'Authenticity' emerged, especially in Modernist fiction and on, as a challenge to the hollowness of sincerity. Authenticity involves a more 'strenuous moral experience' (1972: 11). Trilling's sense of it derives from his idea (in *Beyond Culture* and elsewhere) that 'serious art ... stands ... in an adversary relation to the dominant culture' (1972: 67). To strive for authenticity is to move in the direction of trying to locate an essential self uncompromised by social and cultural pressures, and one that repudiates 'the attenuation of selfhood that results from imperson-ation' (1972: 67). Trilling thinks that literature in general has tended to foster sincerity rather than authenticity. Only the novel has any prospect of restoring individuals to authentic moral health. In part, this is owing to its complex formal possibilities, anti-conventional origins, and poten-tially oppositional stance.

literature (with the exception of the novel, as we saw above), and espe-cially the theatre, for encouraging impersonation and the attenuation of authentic selfhood. For Nietzsche, authenticity involves moving beyond the empty consolations of sincerity, with its illusions and lies, and towards a taking hold of experience with all the pain and suffering it involves. Keats anticipates this way of thinking for Trilling:

> In 1819 Keats said in one of his most memorable letters, 'Do you not see how necessary a World of Pains and troubles is to school an Intelligence and make it a soul?', that is to say, an ego or self which, as he puts it, is 'destined to possess the sense of Identity'.
>
> (Trilling 1972: 166)

In Freud's *Civilization and Its Discontents*, finally, the civilized, con-strained, and repressed personality is shown as being under siege from the primal, anti-social, elements of being that Trilling ultimately wants to privilege. As we move to the world of Booth's moral thinking, we shall quickly become aware of the radical difference between his perspectives and those of James and Trilling. These three American theorists occupy common ground; but they often do very different things on it.

LOLITA AND THE MORAL DIMENSIONS OF BOOTH'S *THE RHETORIC OF FICTION*

Whereas morality is subordinate to aesthetic concerns for James, it is a realm for Trilling that the novel should oppose, attempt to over-come, and transcend. It will hardly be a surprise when I repeat that for Booth morality and ethics are at the core of his theories of fiction. At the forefront of Booth's thinking is his contention that 'the novel comes into existence as something communicable' (1961: 397). He rejects any form of fiction that threatens the clarity of that communi-cation or, by being ambiguous or uncertain about its own moral values, hinders the reader from evaluating her position in relation to the fictional world being constructed. He admired the Russian novelist Dostoevsky (1821–81) because 'not genuine ambiguity, but rather complexity with clarity, seems to be his secret' (1961: 130–31); and he despised Vladimir Nabokov's novel *Lolita* (1955) precisely because it muddied the moral water.

Lolita is the story of Humbert Humbert's sexual relationship with a twelve-year-old girl and his murder of the man she eventually moves on to. It caused a storm at the time of its publication in Paris (1955) and it did not appear in the US until 1958, after which Trilling reviewed it under the title 'The Last Lover' (1958). Trilling acknow-ledges that *Lolita* 'is indeed a shocking book' (1958). But for Trilling, within the context of *The Opposing Self* and *Beyond Culture*, this is praise rather than condemnation: the value of a novel consists almost entirely in its ability to oppose, resist, and go beyond moral platitudes. Trilling situates this 'occasion for outrage' (1958: 332) by declaring that '*Lolita* is about love . . . not about sex' (1958: 334); and 'love requires a scandal' (1958: 337). If culture and social conventions result in impersonation and affectations of sincerity rather than self-hood, Trilling further argues that marriage (as one of the supreme social conventions) can be opposed by 'passion-love'. What appeals to Trilling is Nabokov's mockery of the 'progressive rationalism' (or liberalism) that brought 'the madness of love to an end' (1958: 340). Adultery has lost its oppositional, transgressive force; in fact, it has become a very conventional way of trying to be unconventional. Nabokov, who is on the side of a 'moral mobility' (Trilling 1958: 342) not that distantly related to James's flexible 'moral consciousness' (James 1867: 17), projected a scandalous relationship in order to reinvigorate and dramatize the power of love. This way of reading the novel is entirely consistent with Trilling's concept of 'moral realism': *Lolita* cannot be judged as good or bad for it is good-and-bad; and that 'bad' has its culture-stirring uses.

For Booth, Humbert Humbert is a classic example of an unreliable narrator. This would have been a less unsatisfactory situation if the novel had a clear moral position incorporated in its implied author. 'The history of unreliable narrators from *Gargantua* to *Lolita*', writes Booth, 'is in fact full of traps for the unsuspecting reader, some of them not particularly harmful but some of them crippling or even fatal' (1961: 239). Humbert Humbert is a fatal rather than a cripplingly unreliable narrator. He is an 'indeterminately unreliable narrator' (1961: 315); he is not 'dependable' (as some 'unreliable narrators' are) because he is not 'dependent' (1961: 300n); dependent, that is, on an implied author who can offer a fictional world (of which the unreliable narrator is only a part), so enabling the reader to accept or reject it, to understand and then overstand. The requirement for clear and consistent communication rules out Trilling's 'moral realism' in *The Rhetoric of Fiction*. Concepts such as 'good-and-bad', and the ambiguities they involve, are anathema there:

> When Lionel Trilling confessed recently his inability to decide, in reading Nabokov's controversial *Lolita*, whether the narrator's final indictment of his own immorality is to be taken seriously or ironically, he hastened to explain that this ambiguity made the novel better, not worse.
>
> (Booth 1961: 371)

Booth is unequivocal: 'an author has an obligation to be as clear about his moral position as he possibly can be' (1961: 389). As we shall discover, this is also the view taken, but with some modifications, in *The Company We Keep*.

BOOTH'S *THE COMPANY WE KEEP*

How we judge novels at the levels of quality and moral integrity is at the centre of *The Company We Keep*. This should not involve making confident, once-and-for-all-time judgements, but a 'fluid conversation about the company we keep – and the company that we ourselves provide' (Booth 1988a: x). In this book, Booth extends his notion of the novel as an act of communication further than in *The Rhetoric of Fiction*; it is an act that entails a much more detailed set of responsibilities for both the author and the reader; the emphasis is now on the reader's relations with other readers and not just on that between author and reader. What Booth focuses on in particular is an 'ethical criticism of narrative' and an 'ethics of telling and listening' (1988a: 7). 'Moral judgements', (1988a: 8) such as condemning a novel for recommending murder as socially acceptable, are only a small part of 'the entire range of effects on the "character" or "person" or "self"' (1988a: 8) in which Booth is interested. Booth devotes much of *The Company We Keep* to the need for 'ethical readers'; that is, readers who 'will behave responsibly toward the text' (1988a: 9). Some of this ground was covered in our discussions of 'understanding' and 'overstanding' in the previous chapter.

Two aspects of *The Company We Keep* are particularly relevant to this chapter: Booth's insistence on the 'writer's responsibility to the implied author' (1988a: 128), and his careful (if far from convincing) disavowal of 'simple doctrinal tests' (1988a: 377) when it comes to exercising moral judgements. Booth does not approve of flesh-and-blood writers who distance themselves from their implied authors. The responsibility of authors to their implied authors is 'to write fictions that require the creation of the cleverest, wisest, most generously committed ethos imaginable' (1988a: 128). This takes us back to his ultimate condemnation of 'unreliable narrators' in *The Rhetoric of Fiction*. On the second aspect, Booth argues that we cannot judge *Lolita* to be a bad novel simply by referring to a doctrine (that paedophilia is evil, for example). We need to engage in what he calls 'coduction'. But would Booth have accepted a 'coduced' reading of *Lolita* if a favourable judgement of its 'shocking' subject had been the result? I think not. In the beginning, and in the end, despite his seeming rejection of 'simple doctrinal tests' for establishing 'absolute judgments' (1988a: 377), he is committed to the belief that the moral is equivalent to the human (this is precisely what Trilling denies, of course) and that there is a kind of moral DNA that shapes what it is to be human. Booth concedes, writing in the pragmatist tradition, that 'all statements of truth are partial' (Booth 1988a: 345), and that there is a 'plurality of workable answers' (Booth 1988a: 269). But these are predicated, as we shall see in the final section below, on some fairly sweeping assumptions.

COMPARING JAMES, TRILLING, AND BOOTH ON MORALITY

For James, 'moral intelligence' is broadly equivalent to the artistic sense: if the latter is powerful and responsive enough, it will take care of the former. James would have agreed with Trilling's unease in the presence of narrowly conventional moral thinking, as does Booth to a degree. James also believed that in a world where we only possess partial truths at best, there can be no absolute morality. But Trilling goes beyond James and Booth. He wants novels to resist a category such as the moral, denying as it does the existence of vital, oppositional, realms within the self and beyond culture. Fundamentally, Booth believes that the categories of right and wrong are universal ones.

ABSOLUTE, RELATIVE, AND PRAGMATIC MORALITY

An absolute moralist believes that there should, and can, be no disagreement about what is right and wrong (or good and bad) and that the division between the two rests on universal, cross-cultural principles. Relative moralists stress that different social and historical contexts give rise to different, constantly changing rules. What is right in one context, country, or period, may be deemed wrong in another. The pragmatist holds the view that no one person ever has more than a limited perspective on the truth. Together, we have partial truths and we need to communicate with each other in order to achieve a consensus. This consensus will have to acknowledge that moral principles operate within an experiential context. It is our navigation of, and negotiation with, experience that determines moral principles that will be determined to a large degree by how useful they are. It follows that there will always be a number of ways of thinking about our moral and social responsibilities. Booth has elements of the absolute and the pragmatic in his mix, and none of the relative. Trilling, at times, is a relativist to the point of wanting to attack the very notion of morality as conventionally defined. For James, refining our intelligence in the realm of an art responsive to the shifting and uncertain nature of our experience is the main goal. There are clear features of pragmatism, then, in his position.

There are certain principles that obtain in all cultures for all time (such as, with *Lolita* in mind, it is wrong for a man to have sex with a twelve-year-old girl and then murder his rival). This universalism makes him fairly prescriptive towards the end of *The Rhetoric of Fiction* about the perils of unreliable narration and the ambiguity to which it gives rise. Booth's emphasis throughout *The Company We Keep* is on the need for establishing common rhetorical ground, and on the importance of understanding before we overstand and oppose.

Yet, much of the discussion in *The Rhetoric of Fiction* and *The Company We Keep* takes place within the context of some hefty universalist assumptions: the processes of communication, and of understanding and overstanding, are common to all cultures now and throughout history; that we can (or should) agree on the need for communication, a need to which fiction should be subordinated; and that there is much common ground (however partially we occupy it) about what is right and wrong. Above all, the novel should be an act of clear communication, and Booth feels it important that we both agree on that and accept that concepts such as 'clarity' and 'communication' are more or less intuitive and unchallengeable. Booth takes it for granted that we can talk about the 'universality of our experience of narrative' (1988a: 40). If we challenge this assumption, and in the process contest the very idea of 'universality', the entire edifice of his argument is in danger of collapsing.

SUMMARY

For James, Trilling, and Booth, then, moral issues (variably defined) are at the centre of their theories of the novel. But although they all have the same alphabet, they often speak very different languages. James believes that exercised with rare imagination and taste, the art of fiction cannot but be moral. It does not follow that the writer has to represent vice and evil in all its lurid detail. That would be tasteless (and we can imagine his levelling that kind of accusation at Nabokov's *Lolita*). 'Intelligence' at its height subsumes 'moral intelligence'. To possess a refined and responsive consciousness in the world of experience is to be able to navigate within and beyond conventional moral territory. What connects James and Trilling is their common belief in the novel as the most effective vehicle for representing and interrogating social and moral experience. In the process, for both theorists, it is the means by which individual readers can question moral assumptions. Trilling goes a step further, however. He sees the strength of the novel as being in its potential as an oppositional force. Social and moral norms can cramp, distort, and attenuate authentic selfhood. To an extent he agrees with Rousseau that society and its culture falsifies essentially what we are: a turmoil of primal, often incoherent, forces. The renewal of culture, the very health of society, depends on the maintenance and renovation of the self that novels at their best can produce. Booth is committed to the idea that to be human is to be moral and social. We only possess partial truths at best (which is not the same thing as believing that all morality is relative) and need to 'coduce', or negotiate with others, our moral perspectives. Novels need to be written and read responsibly. This involves trying to understand a writer's intentions (as we saw in the last chapter) and revising our sense of those intentions in conversation with others (which includes reading critical material, of course). Ultimately, although Booth denies that rigid doctrine is a suitable point of reference, he does hold to the idea that judgements about what is right and wrong, or good and bad, derive from the universal condition of being human. This leads him into rejecting complex, ambiguous, novels that fail to make their fictional worlds coherent and their moral positions clear.

AFTER JAMES, TRILLING, AND BOOTH

The critical and theoretical work of Henry James was both the culmination of later nineteenth-century explorations of the craft of fiction and the beginning of twentieth-century ways of thinking about the novel. Consolidating and building on the technical consciousness of nineteenth-century French and Russian novelists such as Flaubert and Turgenev, James initiated an enthusiasm for theorizing about the writing of fiction in the Transatlantic world that has gone on unabated. The purpose of the first section of this chapter is to survey aspects of James's legacy and the current state of play. The second section will work in conjunction with the chapter on 'Further Reading' as a guide to your future study and research on these three theorists of the novel. Trilling and Booth came after James, of course; and as James is one of the progenitors of each, what comes after them also comes (naturally enough) after James. The first section has an 'After James' focus. In the second, some particularly significant work (mainly of the last two or three decades) will be touched on as a way of illustrating not only James's long reach, but dimensions of the legacies specific to Trilling and Booth.

THE SEVEN PHASES OF JAMES'S LEGACY

First of all, there is the immediate (and rather negative) impact of how James's work was interpreted. The American critic Joseph Warren

Beach's *The Method of Henry James* appeared in 1918 (within two years of Henry James's death). This rigidly schematic analysis and expropriation of James's theories of the point of view and centres of consciousness fed directly into the formalism of the New Critics in the 1940s and 1950s. It appeared in a revised and extended edition in 1954 as New Criticism was beginning to dominate the college and university teaching of English in America and beyond. Beach's *The Twentieth-Century Novel: Studies in Technique* (1932) makes even wider claims for James as the prophet of author-elimination in novels. Whereas Beach was influential in the American context, the English writer Percy Lubbock's *The Craft of Fiction* (1921) has had a wide influence both there and in the Anglophone world generally. As with Beach, Lubbock's approach to the theory and practice of fiction is progressivist: James is offered as an example of the high state of evolution in both domains. After what he regarded as the plague of omniscient narration in the nineteenth century, Lubbock welcomed James as a novelist practising and advocating a dramatic method in which obtrusive narration is kept to a minimum and the emphasis is on scenic presentation. Although Lubbock gives far too reductive an interpretation of James's complex and shifting positions, he has in turn been misread. Undoubtedly, his preference is for novels that come as close as possible to drama; and he certainly overestimated the extent to which this is possible. But he also conceded (unlike Beach, and in an anticipation of Booth) that narrators cannot and should not be eliminated.

In the late 1920s and into the 1930s (in the second phase) at a time when Britain and America were experiencing the 'Great Depression' and its consequent social and economic turmoil, James lost his foothold in America. Slightly earlier, Van Wyck Brooks (1925) accepted Beach's and Lubbock's overemphasis on James's formalism and argued that it was a result of his self-imposed European exile; this technical preoccupation was at odds with Brook's own preference for the socially and politically engaged fiction championed by Vernon Parrington (1927–30) and others. Ironically, given its commitment to Marxism, it was the *Partisan Review* that began to field articles in the later 1930s and 1940s (the third phase) arguing for the social and political relevance of James's work. See, for example, the essays on Henry James reprinted in Rahv (1969). F. O. Matthiessen, a fierce proponent of communism at the time, published *Henry James: The Major Phase* in 1944. It remains one of the leading books on James's work and formed part of the platform on which Lionel Trilling was to stand. In *The Liberal Imagination* (1950), *The Opposing Self* (1955b), and *Beyond Culture* (1965), Trilling went against the growing formalist spirit of the times and emphasized the political dimensions of James's novels and the moral relevance (defined in a Jamesian way as an awareness of how complex the moral life is) of James's fiction and theories of fiction. Formalism, in its New Critical manifestation, gained ground as Marxism with its insistence on socially relevant fiction lost its way. Trilling's *The Liberal Imagination* is, in part, an attempt to offer a compromise: social commitment matters; but so does a willingness to resist simple ways of looking at life's complications. The mark of Henry James (as Trilling openly acknowledges) can be seen everywhere in this kind of approach.

By the time of Booth's *The Rhetoric of Fiction* (1961), open war was beginning to break out between the humanistic approaches of critics such as Lionel Trilling and the scientific methods of New Critical analysis. The New Critics were much more interested in poetry than in prose fiction or novels. But the anthology and textbook, *Understanding Fiction* (Brooks and Warren 1943), which was modelled on their hugely influential *Understanding Poetry* (1938), was published in 1943. Its assumptions, in line with the territory mapped out in James's 'The Art of Fiction' (James 1884) and New York prefaces (1907–9), were organicist. The idea that form and content were not only closely related but indistinguishable was hardly unique to James; but the New Critics often claimed a license for their position in James's criticism, especially the New York prefaces, which had been published in one extremely influential volume (*The Art of the Novel*) edited by Blackmur in 1934. In identifying, or imposing, a network of contradictions and tensions ultimately formally resolved in each novel (Van Ghent 1953 is the classic study here), these critics went way beyond James. However pure an art he pursued, James remained committed to the novel's powers of intervention in the world of social and moral experience. Into this breach between form and values stepped Booth as he attempted to reconcile the two. In *The Rhetoric of Fiction*, one of his main aims is to rescue James from the clutches of formalism so that he can be restored to the moral and ethical realm. As it turns out, of course, he discovers that James is only partly fit for such a purpose, not least because of his celebration of technical features such as unreliable narration. Ironically, Booth is still known for the explosion of interest he created in the form and technique of narration rather than for his focus on values. Here begins the fifth phase.

From the late 1960s through to the 1970s and a little beyond, the fever was for narratology and structuralism. For this reason, Trilling was neglected (or attacked) during this period; only in the later twentieth century and after has there been a return to books such as *Sincerity and Authenticity* and to the continuing historical importance of *The Liberal Imagination*, *The Opposing Self*, and *Beyond Culture* as historians and cultural critics try to account for and theorize the counter-cultural movement of the 1960s, structuralism, and post-structuralism. To a large degree, as far as the genre of the novel is concerned, structuralism (however different the language and terms it deployed) was much the same as narratology. Both were deeply indebted to the formalism of the New Critics and to the significance James placed on the formal and technical side of narratives. But if the New Critics took works apart so that they could be reassembled and admired in all their unified perfection, narratologists were much more interested in how stories were told. The distinction between what was told, the content (broadly), and how (what used to be called the form), has been pursued much more strenuously by structuralists. By contrast with Booth, and with a number of narratologists (see Prince 1982), structuralists have not been primarily interested in the novel as an act of communication. Central to their approach is the question 'How?' The question 'Why?' – or the whole context of purpose and value – was never an issue for them.

If phase five of the James legacy is broadly structuralist and phase seven (there will be more about this in the next section) 'after theory', post-structuralism is phase six. Structuralists, such as the New Critics (and James to an extent) regarded texts as systems, unified structures, or wholes. Post-structuralists reject the stability of the text, and its system of relations, proposed by structuralists. Texts cannot be regarded as machines for generating interpretations; and meaning, or significance, is unattainable in a world where one thing always leads to another. James's emphasis, in theory and practice, on the endless deferral of meaning, and on the mismatch between language and what it purports to describe, means that his work has often been recruited by post-structuralist theorists (see Rowe 1984).

SOME RECENT LANDMARK WORK IN THE
JAMES, TRILLING, AND BOOTH MOULD

In this section, I want to focus on a sequence of more recent developments on sites first occupied by James, Trilling, and Booth in order to demonstrate the continuing currency of their theories of the novel. This is a highly selective account; but I shall mention other relevant work in passing.

The concepts James developed and the forms of attention he applied to the criticism of the novel have continued to exercise a strong influence on major studies of the novel and narrative method in recent years. Much of this work has taken place around theories of the point of view. Dorrit Cohn's *Transparent Minds: Narrative Modes for Presenting Consciousness in Fiction* (1978) indicates, by its very title, the degree to which it has as its departure point aspects of narrative and representation that are at the core of James's approach. Cohn's preoccupation is with 'free indirect speech', or what she calls 'narrated monologue', and her study identifies Flaubert, Zola, and James as preparing the ground for these techniques by foregrounding consciousness, or subjectivity, in the novel. If narrated monologue, as Cohn argues, established a bridge between nineteenth- and twentieth-century fiction, James is one of its principal architects. It is worth noting that whatever sophistications Cohn introduces in the realm of presenting consciousness, she minimizes James's complex sense of the relations between consciousness and narration. James is not only Cohn's predecessor; he fully anticipates her concepts.

Ann Banfield, in her *Unspeakable Sentences: Narration and Representation in the Language of Fiction* (1982), locates herself in much the same territory as Dorrit Cohn. But she challenges the idea (which is at the centre of Booth's *The Rhetoric of Fiction*) that free indirect speech, or third-person point of view narration, are forms of communication, telling, or speech. She insists on the extent to which the point of view in fiction can become quite independent of any particular speaker and emphasizes that neither the sentences of narration nor sentences representing consciousness can be found in the spoken language. These are literary, not spoken, manifestations (hence the 'speakerless sentences' of the title). Banfield, however (like Cohn), finds herself underestimating the sophistication of James's approach in order, however inadvertently, to heighten the originality of her own work. James does not make the rigid distinction between 'telling' and 'showing' she imagines (there is too much of a reliance on James's mis-interpreters such as Lubbock and Beach here) as our discussion in Chapter 4 of the preface to *What Maisie Knew* demonstrated.

More specific work on point of view includes Lanser (1981) and Weimann (1984). Weimann berates Booth for failing to concentrate sufficiently on the 'social and psychological forces that affect authors and readers' (1984: 250). Earlier, Uspensky (1973) tried to tackle this neglect by subdividing point of view into four categories: 'phraseological' (at the level of language, or telling), 'ideological', 'psychological', and 'spatial'. This 'spatial' dimension corresponds in part with Genette's 'focalization', a term that Bal (1985) partitions into 'focalizer' and 'focalized' (the object of the focalization). Ross (1976), despite Booth and Genette, considers the process whereby characters become narrators by disregarding almost entirely undramatized narrators or narrative voices. Friedman (1975) has produced one of the most systematic accounts of point of view; but as with Ross's, it represents a regression from Booth in that he pays little attention to 'reliability, distance, tone, and the author-reader relationship' (Lanser 1981: 28).

One of the themes of this book has been the extent to which moral thinking is central to the theories of fiction held by James, Trilling, and Booth. As we saw from the earlier part of this chapter, New Critics and structuralists alike tended to quarantine the issue of values from James's theories of narrative. If Booth offered one corrective to this approach, more recently, Martha C. Nussbaum's *Love's Knowledge: Essays on Philosophy and Literature* (1990) is another. Nussbaum recognizes the importance of organic form in James and has no problem in acknowledging the interdependence of form and content in novels. For Nussbaum – as for James, the New Critics, Trilling (to an extent), and Booth – 'form and style are not incidental features' of the text (Nussbaum 1990: 5–6). Nussbaum rejects Banfield's notion that narratives consist of 'speakerless sentences'. Nussbaum is on the same track as Booth here. He reminded his readers in 1984 that 'there is no such thing as a fictional form that is value-free' (Booth 1984: xvi–xvii).

Against the grain of structuralist and post-structuralist denials of 'voice' in narrative (Gibson 1996: 166), Nussbaum argues that 'a view of life is *told* in fiction', and that '[l]ife is never simply *presented* by a text' (Nussbaum 1990: 5). Nussbaum builds on and develops further

Booth's concept of the implied author as she reflects on a question everywhere posed in Henry James's novel, *The Ambassadors* (1903): 'How should one live?' (Nussbaum 1990: 36). Booth's *The Rhetoric of Fiction* and his *The Company We Keep*, are concerned not just with the novel's impact on how we live, but with the ethics of reading. Nussbaum holds to the view that novels are an important intervention at the practical level in our moral lives. Like Trilling and James, in words they could have written, for Nussbaum 'the novel is committed more deeply than many other forms to a multiplicity and fineness' of 'distinctions'; 'novels', she argues, 'show us the worth and richness of plural qualitative thinking' (1990: 36). Practical wisdom (or moral thinking in action) requires the impetus of emotion that novel-reading can supply. Nussbaum has little time for narrative theories that confine themselves to the question of how a text works: her energy is devoted to such issues as purpose and affect.

The oppositional self, especially within a Freudian paradigm, is crucial to Trilling's novel criticism and overall cultural project. Selves, for Trilling (as for Freud), emerge in opposition to the culture, or society, that wrenches and distorts them into civilization and compliance. What Trilling admires about the novel at its best is its refractoriness, its resistance to culture; when readers seek to preserve, rather than eradicate, its rough grain, they can be regenerated by reading fiction. Nussbaum pursues this idea in the direction of moral philosophy.

The French theorist Marthe Robert keeps Freud, or Trilling's Freud, firmly in sight. In *Origins of the Novel* (1980), Robert characterizes the novel as an 'upstart' (1980: 57), arguing that whereas 'traditional forms' are subject to 'prescriptions and proscriptions', the novel (as James and Trilling believe) 'knows neither rule nor restraint' (1980: 58). 'During the whole of its history', Robert continues, 'the novel has derived the violence of its desires and its irrepressible freedom from the Family Romance' (1980: 167). If children struggle towards imagination and freedom after an early admiration of their parents, the novel, similarly, is founded on rebellion and lawlessness. Robert's account is stimulating and provocative because it accepts the relevance of Freud's family romance to the themes of many novels but goes beyond the merely thematic: it is part of the way in which she traces the very emergence of the novel and its subsequent development.

FAMILY ROMANCE

There are three stages of development for the individual in Freud's 'family romance'. (1) The child admires and seeks to emulate her parents. (2) This turns to rebellion as other parents seem superior. (3) The child begins to believe that she is illegitimate, and to fantasize about who her real parents might be. Robert sees the novel going through these three stages (and (3) corresponds with the arrival of the imagination necessary for its production) in relation to poetry and the drama. The analogy, then, is between the novel and those resisting selves celebrated by Trilling.

Three years after the translation of Robert's *Origins of the Novel* appeared, a second edition of Booth's *The Rhetoric of Fiction* (1983a) was published. Booth's 'Afterword' amounts to a highly significant intervention on his own site; and it helps us to see what he regards as being some of the satisfactory, and less satisfactory, developments and extensions of his work on fiction. Since the first edition in 1961, structuralism had come and gone, more or less, and narratology no longer remained supreme (as Nussbaum and Robert demonstrate in different ways). Despite post-structuralist attacks on the idea of essentialism, and on the possibility of universal values or forms of communication, Booth still holds to the claim that 'rhetorical inquiry is universally applicable' (1983a: 405). Narratology uncovers narratives everywhere in life and art: and Booth regrets that his concentration on fiction in 1961 obscured this prevalence. He further regrets (with structuralism hovering) the lack of any real emphasis on language and style in the first edition of *The Rhetoric of Fiction*. But he remains adamant that, despite contemporary theoretical views to the contrary (see Rimmon-Kenan 1983), characters are not '*made of* language'; they are 'imagined people' (Booth 1983a: 409).

In the face of a good deal of subsequent criticism on the moral stance he took in *The Rhetoric of Fiction*, Booth reinforces his sense of the importance of morals and ethics when it comes to the writing and reading of fiction. But he concedes that his rejection of ambiguity as 'fog' in 1961 (1961: 372) was a little (so to speak) short-sighted. Although reluctant to embrace narrative confusion wholeheartedly, Booth considers the contribution to this issue of the American narratologist Peter J. Rabinowitz (1977). Rabinowitz is the first of a number of theorists whose departure point (at least in part) is *The Rhetoric of Fiction* and whose ideas Booth assesses in his 'Afterword'. The others are Seymour Chatman (1978), who was one of the critics responsible for introducing structuralist theories of narrative to America, his fellow editor on the journal *Critical Inquiry*, Sheldon Sacks (1964), and Gérard Genette (1980).

Rabinowitz's distinction between a 'narrative audience', an 'authorial audience', and the flesh-and-blood reader, informs Booth's *The Company We Keep*. In the second edition of *The Rhetoric of Fiction*, Booth admits that the tension in 'belief systems' (1983a: 424) of these three groups can be pleasurable and not just confusing and immoral: 'I am threatened only by *some* foggy landscapes; others I enjoy' (1983a: 425). The 'narrative audience', reading credulously as if absorbed in the real world, gets caught up in the 'unavoidable complexities and irresolutions that can be called ambiguities' (1983a: 425). But there is another kind of ambiguity that Booth is not prepared to tolerate so easily: that is when we cannot work out which of a variety of narrative audience positions we are supposed to accept. Do we regard the governess in James's *The Turn of the Screw*, for example (again), as innocent or vicious? Although this kind of ambiguity, as Booth steps back from the strictures of *The Rhetoric of Fiction*, is not necessarily to be deplored, the 'Afterword' still questions the 'curiously fashionable assumption that ambiguities are in themselves always valuable' (1983a: 426).

Both Sheldon Sacks (1964) and Gérard Genette (1980) work in seams mined earlier by Booth, among others. Booth, in fact, is quite keen to claim that Genette's distinction between *l'histoire* and *récit*, which is very close to Seymour Chatman's (1978) between discourse and story, adds little to the central argument of *The Rhetoric of Fiction*. Booth specifies two levels of the text there: events, and the way in which they are told or transformed. This, he believes, is the same duality detailed by Chatman and Genette. Perhaps: but Booth has a different way of thinking about how they interact. He has little difficulty in conceiving characters and events in isolation from the story-telling that nevertheless shapes them. For Chatman and Genette, however, the story (the entire content of the narrative, including characters, events, settings, and the like) can only be isolated

DISCOURSE AND STORY

Broadly speaking, 'discourse' is the means by which the 'story' is transmitted. The events, characters, and setting (the 'story': which is not to be
confused with plot, or with the popular sense of what is meant by a story)
are arranged at the level of discourse (see Chatman 1978). In Conrad's
The Heart of Darkness, Kurtz is a character and part of the story; he is
represented in the discourse through Marlowe's narrative. Conrad might
have chosen to use an undramatized, third-person, narrator. This would
have been a different discourse for the same story. Similarly, if *Heart
of Darkness* were transposed into a film, the story would still include
Kurtz as a character; but the discourse would be the medium of the film.
For Chatman, discourse and story are only separable for analytical
purposes. There can be no character, for example, unless he or she has
a transmitting discourse.

from the discourse (the transmission and arrangement of the story)
for the purposes of analysis. There can be no discourse-free character
or event.

   Booth admires what is probably Genette's most distinctive contribution to narrative theory: his 'systematic account' of the
'interrelations between the material time scheme and realized narrative time' (Booth 1983a: 439). Between, that is, how much time is
passing and how much text it takes to convey that passing time. But
ultimately, what is missing for Booth in Genette is an attention to
fiction as a communication of values. He finds this abundantly in
Sheldon Sacks's *Fiction and the Shape of Belief*; although he sees Sacks as
having too small an appetite for the technical elements of narrative.
Booth wants to re-unite the intertwining strands of value and technique bequeathed by James, and squandered by critics who have
subjected them to futile disentanglement:

> If one could by some magical stroke incorporate the virtues of other books
> into one's own, the two that would be most helpful in this regard are
> Sheldon Sack's *Fiction and the Shape of Belief* and Gérard Genette's *Narrative
> Discourse.*

(Booth 1983a: 438)

Genette followed up his *Narrative Discourse* (1980) with *Narrative Discourse Revisited* (1988). He tackles there some of the points made in Booth's 'Afterword', and questions the need for the concept of an implied author.

A year after the second edition of *The Rhetoric of Fiction* was published, Booth's introduction to an English translation of the Russian critic Mikhail Bakhtin's (1895–1975) *Problems of Dostoyevsky's Poetics* appeared; and Bakhtin was set to become immensely fashionable in the last two decades of the twentieth century. *Problems of Dostoyevsky's Poetics* was first published in Russian in 1929, but Booth was unaware of it when writing in the late 1950s. One of Bakhtin's most important ideas is that novels are dialogical, not monological. The self is not a simple unity: it is constituted by many different voices. There are many voices in play in a novel, and these cannot be congealed into one 'authorial' register. In fact, they often fight against any one view that tries to prevail in a text. Booth has to acknowledge the challenge to the entire argument of *The Rhetoric of Fiction*: 'the unity of the work' cannot 'be identified with the total choices of the implied author . . . The author will have "disappeared" from the work' (Booth 1984: xxiii). Booth's immediate reaction is to suggest that Bakhtin's argument works well for Dostoyevsky, but that it might not do so elsewhere. He also argues that the sum total of all the techniques a writer uses in any one novel to free his characters from authorial control into dialogy operate on a superior level to the rest of the text, the level on which Booth seeks to locate his implied author. There is no doubt, however, that Bakhtin had a profound impact on Booth's thinking. When allied with post-structuralist denials of monology, and of authority in general, it raises serious questions about the assumptions (relating to unity and authorial control) made by Booth's conceptual model.

CONCLUSION

Henry James made at least two enduring contributions to the theory of the novel: he succeeded in establishing it as a worthy object of critical attention by lifting it to the level of an art; and in 'The Art of Fiction' and the New York edition prefaces in particular, he helped to initiate discussions about structure, narrative method, representation, moral thinking, and interpretation that continue to exert a powerful influence on contemporary literary criticism. Lionel Trilling built on the moral and social dimensions of James's writing to foster a role for himself as a cultural critic at a time when the New Critics were becoming obsessed with form and technique. These are the two strands that Booth attempts to re-unite in *The Rhetoric of Fiction*. The work surveyed in the last section demonstrates the continuing significance of James, Trilling, and Booth.

FURTHER READING

There are four sections to this further reading guide: Henry James, Lionel Trilling, Wayne C. Booth, and General. In the General section, works relevant to all three writers will be cited; but there will be some overlap, of course, in the first three sections.

HENRY JAMES

WORKS BY JAMES

A comprehensive collection of James's literary criticism can be found in:

Essays on Literature, American Writers, English Writers. Literary Criticism (1984), Vol. 1, Library of America, New York: Literary Classics of the United States, Inc.; *French Writers, Other European Writers, The Prefaces to the New York Edition. Literary Criticism* (1984), Vol. 2, Library of America, New York: Literary Classics of the United States, Inc. The first volume contains all the wide-ranging essays (such as 'The Art of Fiction'); the rest of the material is organized by author, alphabetically, and chronologically within each author section. The second volume includes the prefaces to the New York Edition.

Henry James on Culture: Collected Essays on Politics and the American Social Scene (1999) ed. Pierre A. Walker, Lincoln, NE and London: University of Nebraska Press.

These essays are not on fiction and the novel, but they are a valuable insight into some of James's wider political and social concerns (and they are mostly excluded from the Library of America edition).

Theory of Fiction: Henry James (1972) ed. James E. Miller Jr, Lincoln, NE and London: University of Nebraska Press.

A useful extraction of James's critical essays that is arranged thematically.

It can be helpful to develop a sense of how James arranged his own critical and theoretical essays and to see the sequence in which they appeared. The following list will enable you to do this:

French Poets and Novelists (1878) London: Macmillan and Co.

Hawthorne (1879; 1999) ed. Kate Fullbrook, Nottingham: Trent editions.

Partial Portraits (1888), London and New York: Macmillan and Co.

This contains a slightly revised version of 'The Art of Fiction' (1884).

Essays in London and Elsewhere (1893) London: James R. Osgood, McIlvaine & Co.

There are two particularly significant essays in this collection: 'Gustave Flaubert' (1893) and 'Criticism' (which first appeared as 'The Science of Criticism' in 1891).

Picture and Text (1893) New York: Harper and Brothers.

Prefaces to The Novels and Tales of Henry James: 'New York Edition' (1907–09), New York: Charles Scribner's Sons.

Notes on Novelists (1914), London: J. M. Dent & Sons

This volume includes, among others, a second essay on Flaubert (1902), and essays on Robert Louis Stevenson (1894), Émile Zola (1902), Balzac (1902 and 1913), George Sand (1897, 1899, and 1914), and 'The New Novel' (1914).

WORKS ON JAMES

There is a vast amount of criticism on Henry James. Necessarily, this is an extremely selective list. The aim is to highlight material that will be particularly helpful within the context of the themes and issues of this book.

Blackmur, Richard P. (1934) Introduction to *The Art of the Novel: Critical Prefaces by Henry James*, New York: Scribner.

Blackmur's collection has become so influential that it is often cited simply under 'Henry James'. The introduction summarizes the key feature of each preface.

Daugherty, Sarah B. (1981) *The Literary Criticism of Henry James*, Athens, OH: Ohio University Press.

A solid mapping of the territory.

Falk, Richard P. (1955) 'The Literary Criticism of the Genteel Decades, 1870–1900', in Floyd Stovall (ed.) *The Development of American Literary Criticism*, New Haven, CT: College and University Press.

Concentrates (with James at its centre) on the three decades when James produced a substantial amount of literary criticism.

Fergusson, Francis (1943) 'James's Idea of Dramatic Form', *Kenyon Review*, 5: 495–507.

An essay very much in the tradition of Percy Lubbock (in a journal that was mainly an organ for the New Critical position).

Friedman, Norman (1975) *Form and Meaning in Fiction*, Athens, GA: University of Georgia Press.

James is the key protagonist in this historical approach to novel technique and theory.

Goode, John (1966) 'The Art of Fiction: Walter Besant and Henry James', in David Howard, John Lucas, John Goode (eds) *Tradition and Tolerance in Nineteenth-Century Fiction: Critical Essays on Some English and American Novels*, London: Routledge & Kegan Paul: 243–81 (see also Spilka 1973).

Situates 'The Art of Fiction' in its historical context.

Jones, Vivien (1984) *James the Critic*, London: Macmillan.

This is a benchmark book on James's development as a critic. It is particularly good at setting his work in its European (French) context.

Lubbock, Percy (1921) *The Craft of Fiction*, London: Jonathan Cape.
   The classic early study of James's New York Edition prefaces.

McWhirter, David (ed.) (1995) *Henry James's New York Edition: The Construction of Authorship*, Stanford, CA: Stanford University Press.
   McWhirter's collection is monumentally important. Of the sixteen essays, the most groundbreaking is Eve Kosofsky Sedgwick's 'Shame and Performativity: Henry James's New York Edition Prefaces': 206–39.

Marshall, Adré (1998) *The Turn of the Mind: Constituting Consciousness in Henry James*, London: Associated University Presses.
   Marshall tests and contests Dorrit Cohn's (1978) models of narrative within a Jamesian paradigm.

Morrison, Sister Kristin (1961) 'James's and Lubbock's Differing Points of View', *Nineteenth-Century Fiction*, 16: 245–55.
   Examines the mismatch between James's prefaces and Lubbock's interpretation of them.

Nussbaum, Martha C. (1990) *Love's Knowledge: Essays on Philosophy and Literature*, New York and Oxford: Oxford University Press.
   An application, in part, of what Nussbaum takes as being James's integrated approach to morals and narrative method.

Pearson, John H. (1997) *The Prefaces of Henry James: Framing the Modern Reader*, University Park, PA: Pennsylvania State University Press.
   Pearson devotes his energies to James's senses of his readers in the New York Edition prefaces.

Peterson, Dale E. (1975) *The Clement Vision: Poetic Realism in Turgenev and James*, Port Washington, NY and London: Kennikat Press.
   An account of the influence of Turgenev on James's theories of realism and of Turgenev's impact generally on American senses of representation and the novel.

Rawlings, Peter (ed.) (1993) *Critical Essays on Henry James*, Critical Thought Series 5, Aldershot and Brookfield, VT: Scolar Press.
   These essays and reviews were published during James's own lifetime. They indicate the early impact of his critical and theoretical work. Of particular interest is the range of assessments of the New York Edition prefaces.

Rowe, John Carlos (1984) *The Theoretical Dimensions of Henry James*, London: Methuen.

One of the first books to situate James in a structuralist and post-structuralist context.

Rowe, John Carlos (1998) *The Other Henry James*, New Americanists, Durham, NC and London: Duke University Press.

The introduction, 'Henry James and Critical Theory', takes up where Rowe's *The Theoretical Dimensions of Henry James* left off.

Seed, David (1981) 'The Narrator in James's Criticism', *Philological Quarterly* 60: 501–21.

An incisive analysis of James's perspectives on the narrator.

Spilka, Mark (1973) 'Henry James and Walter: "The Art of Fiction" Controversy', in Mark Spilka (ed.) (1977) *Towards a Poetics of Fiction*, Bloomington, IN and London: Indiana University Press: 190–208.

Examines not just the relation between James and Besant, but also Robert Louis Stevenson's reaction to 'The Art of Fiction' (see also Goode 1966).

Ward, J. A. (1967) *The Search for Form*: *Studies in the Structure of James's Fiction*, Chapel Hill, NC: University of North Carolina Press.

The early chapters represent one of the best studies of James's concept of organic form.

Wellek, René (1965) 'Henry James', *A History of Modern Criticism*: *1750–1950*, Vol. 4, *The Later Nineteenth Century*, London: Jonathan Cape: 213–37.

A comprehensive essay which locates James firmly within the New Critical paradigm.

LIONEL TRILLING

WORKS BY TRILLING

Matthew Arnold (1939) New York: Norton; (rev. edn 1949), New York: Columbia University Press.

Trilling's conversion of his Columbia PhD dissertation. Throughout his life, Trilling shared Arnold's emphasis (outlined here) on the social and moral relevance of literature.

E. M. Forster (1943) Norfolk, CT; (rev. edn 1964) New York: New Directions.

The study in which Trilling developed his concept of 'moral realism' (which derives partly from Forster).

The Middle of the Journey (1947) New York: Viking.

Despite his intentions otherwise, Trilling's one and only novel. It explores the plight of disaffected communists in the 1930s and 1940s.

The Liberal Imagination (1950) New York: Viking.

Trilling's most popular and influential collection of essays. Its main purpose is to rescue 'liberalism' from the clutches of Stalinism and Marxism by restoring complexity to the political realm. The genre of the novel (as ever for Trilling) is the chief vehicle of this restoration.

The Opposing Self (1955) New York: Viking.

Building on his enthusiasm for Freud, this collection of essays explores the extent to which the self always emerges in opposition to culture. Among its concerns is what it identifies as the process whereby adversarial literature is often domesticated and rendered timid once it becomes the object of academic study.

Freud and the Crisis of Our Culture (1955) Boston, MA: Beacon.

A Freud Anniversary Lecture. It pursues an argument (consolidated in *The Opposing Self* and continued in *Beyond Culture*) involving Freud's focus on the self as a biological fact beyond culture.

A Gathering of Fugitives (1956) Boston, MA: Beacon.

A collection of essays aimed at the non-academic reader; many of these appeared in *The Griffin*, the monthly magazine of The Reader's Subscription.

Beyond Culture: Essays in Language and Literature (1965) New York: Viking.

An extension of the view first projected in *The Opposing Self* that culture compromises a self whose task is to resist it.

Sincerity and Authenticity (1972) Cambridge, MA: Harvard University Press.

Trilling's history of these two concepts and their interrelationship.

Mind in the Modern World (1973) New York: Viking.

An examination of the tendency of modern culture to diminish the importance of the mind (reprinted in *The Last Decade*, 1979).

The Works of Lionel Trilling, Uniform Editions (1977–80), 12 volumes, New York: Harcourt Brace Jovanovich.

Gathered together as a tribute to her husband by Diana Trilling.

Of This Time, of That Place and Other Stories (1979), selected by Diana Trilling, New York and London: Harcourt Brace Jovanovich.

The first (title) story (much anthologized) is semi-autobiographical: it depicts the experience of a young teacher pitched against a peculiar student.

The Last Decade: *Essays and Reviews*, 1965–75 (1979), ed. Diana Trilling, New York and London: Harcourt Brace Jovanovich.

Essays written by Trilling after *Beyond Culture* (1965); they include the 1973 lecture 'The Mind in the Modern World'.

Prefaces to the Experience of Literature (1979) New York and London: Harcourt Brace Jovanovich.

Trilling's prefaces to the anthology *The Experience of Literature: A Reader with Commentaries* (1967), New York: Holt, Rinehart, and Winston.

Speaking of Literature and Society (1980) ed. Diana Trilling, New York and London: Harcourt Brace Jovanovich.

A volume of previously uncollected writings. As well as later material, it contains many essays written in the 1930s and 1940s for the Jewish periodical *The Menorah Journal* and a number of *Partisan Review* pieces.

The Moral Obligation to be Intelligent: *Selected Essays* (2000) ed. Leon Wieseltier, New York: Farrar, Strauss, Giroux.

An invaluable collection of essays as they first appeared (and before they were revised for subsequent collections).

WORKS ON TRILLING

Anderson, Quentin, Stephen Donadio, and Steven Marcus (eds) (1977) *Art, Politics, and Will: Essays in Honor of Lionel Trilling*, New York: Basic Books.

A volume of essays published shortly after Trilling's death. It is one of the best all-round assessments of his work; this is not least because some of the essays use Trilling as a departure point for new enquiries along his lines. Contributors include Edward Said, Frank Kermode, and Richard Hoggart.

Bloom, Alexander (1986) *Prodigal Sons: The New York Intellectuals and Their World*, New York: Oxford University Press.

Trilling figures in this study as a key member of the New York Intellectuals, and *The Liberal Imagination* as one of its most significant texts. (See also Teres.)

Boyers, Robert (1977) *Lionel Trilling: Negative Capability and the Wisdom of Avoidance*, Columbia, MO and London: University of Missouri Press.

An investigation of Trilling's insistence on complex awareness in relation to the oscillation in his writing (which Boyers also sees in James) between involvement in, and the avoidance of, the world of experience and abstract thinking.

Chace, William M. (1980) *Lionel Trilling: Criticism and Politics*, Stanford, CA: Stanford University Press.

A wide-ranging consideration of Trilling's work focusing, mainly, on the volatile relation there between literature and politics.

Dickstein, Morris (1992) *Double Agent: The Critic and Society*, New York and Oxford: Oxford University Press.

Sees Trilling as pitched against dogmatic politics (such as Stalinism) in the 1940s only to find himself under threat from academic professionalization. Trilling was a double agent in that he attempted to bridge the gap between the professional (academic) critic and the educated reader.

Donoghue, Denis (1978) 'Trilling, Mind, and Society', *Sewanee Review*, 86: 161–86.

Trilling could not help despising the rhetoric of the counter-cultural 1960s; it seemed like a mass-produced version of his own concept of the opposing self.

Frank, Joseph (1956) 'Lionel Trilling and the Conservative Imagination', *Sewanee Review*, 86: 296–309.

Traces what Frank sees as Trilling's movement from critic of the liberal imagination to spokesman for conservative (or neo-conservative) values.

Freedman, Jonathan (1993) 'Trilling, James, and the Uses of Cultural Criticism', *Henry James Review*, 14: 141–50.

Freedman sees Trilling as retrospectively constructing James as an outsider like himself.

French, Phillip (1980) *Three Honest Men: Edmund Wilson, F. R. Leavis, and Lionel Trilling*, Manchester: Carcanet New Press.

Argues that all three writers are concerned not with what literature is, but with what it can (and should) do in the social and moral realms.

Krupnick, Mark (1986) *Lionel Trilling and the Fate of Cultural Criticism*, Evanston, IL: Northwestern University Press.

Trilling's is a politics of the self as he wrestles with his conflicting commitment both to liberal principles and (adversarial) modernist literature.

O'Hara, Daniel T. (1988) *Lionel Trilling: The Work of Liberation*, The Wisconsin Project on American Writers, Madison, WI: University of Wisconsin Press.

A useful account of Trilling's work.

Rawlings, Peter (2001) 'Trilling Unlionised', *Essays in Criticism*, 51: 276–82.

A consideration of the impact of some recent work on Trilling.

Rodden, John (ed.) (1999) *Lionel Trilling and the Critics: Opposing Selves*, Lincoln, NE and London: University of Nebraska Press.

An indispensable collection of essays on Trilling. A major volume in the current re-evaluation of Trilling's past and continuing significance.

Salmagundi (1978) special Trilling issue, 41.

A special journal issue devoted to Trilling three years after his death.

Scholes, Robert (1973) 'The Illiberal Imagination', *New Literary History*, 4: 521–40.

On Trilling and pluralistic thinking.

Schwartz, Delmore (1953) 'The Duchess' Red Shoes', *Partisan Review*, 20: 55–73.

An attack on Trilling in terms of his narrow-minded commitment to the values and attitudes of the educated, middle-class reader.

Scott, Nathan A. (1973) *Three American Moralists: Mailer, Bellow, Trilling*, Notre Dame and London: University of Notre Dame Press.

All three writers are concerned not simply (or at all) with what literature is but with what it does.

Shoben, Edward J. (1981) *Lionel Trilling*, New York: Ungar.

Elaborates on the central importance to Trilling's work of the conflict between self and culture or society.

Simpson, Lewis P. (1987) 'Lionel Trilling and the Agency of Terror', *Partisan Review*, 54: 18–35.

Concentrates on the degree to which Trilling was never more than partially reconciled to working in an academic environment that mutes the terror of literature.

Tanner, Stephen L. (1988) *Lionel Trilling*, Boston, MA: Twayne Publishers.

A solid and comprehensive introduction to Trilling.

Teres, Harvey M. (1996) *Renewing the Left: Politics, Imagination, and the New York Intellectuals*, New York and Oxford: Oxford University Press.

Like Bloom (see above), Teres tries to locate Trilling among the New York Intellectuals; but he concludes that he occupied an uneasy place there. Teres is interesting on Trilling's role in the revival of interest in Henry James during the early 1940s.

Wellek, René (1986) 'Lionel Trilling', in his *A History of Modern Criticism*, Vol. 6, *American Criticism, 1900–1950*, New Haven, CT and London: Yale University Press: 123–43.

An assessment of Trilling's contribution to American literary criticism.

WAYNE C. BOOTH

WORKS BY BOOTH

Booth contributed prolifically to a wide range of periodicals; this can be a list of his key publications only.

The Rhetoric of Fiction (1961; rev. edn 1983) Chicago, IL: Chicago University Press.

Booth's major work and a landmark in the theory of fiction.

Now Don't Try to Reason with Me: Essays and Ironies for a Credulous Age (1970) Chicago, IL: University of Chicago Press.

A book provoked in part by Booth's experience as a Dean at the University of Chicago during the demonstrations and protests in the late 1960s. Booth focuses on the use and abuse of rhetoric.

A Rhetoric of Irony (1974) Chicago, IL: Chicago University Press.

Booth divides irony into two types: stable and unstable. Irony is unstable if it leads to an interpretation that can be further undercut. He emphasizes the importance (problematically) of understanding the writer's intention so that ironies can be stabilized. Where there is uncertainty about what the text means, Booth believes that we should always favour the reading that 'contributes most to the quality of the work' (and he feels confident that it is possible to establish what that quality amounts to).

Modern Dogma and the Rhetoric of Assent (1974) Notre Dame: Notre Dame University Press.

An intervention in the theory of rhetoric in which Booth examines the process of assenting to and denying arguments (especially about values).

Critical Understanding: The Powers and Limits of Pluralism (1979) Chicago, IL: Chicago University Press.

This book argues that there are multiple ways of approaching literary texts but that this is not the same thing as accepting the relativist view that they are all equally valid. Booth attempts to establish common standards against which critical interpretations can be measured.

'Rhetorical Critics Old and New: The Case of Gérard Genette' (1983) in Laurence Lerner (ed.) *Reconstructing Literature*, Oxford: Blackwell: 123–213.

An assessment of Genette's work which criticizes it, ultimately, for not being concerned with values.

'Introduction' (1984) to *Problems of Dostoyevsky's Poetics*, by Mikhail Bakhtin, trans. by Caryl Emerson, Manchester: Manchester University Press: xiii–xxvii.

Booth takes on Bakhtin.

The Company We Keep: An Ethics of Fiction (1988) Berkeley, CA: University of California Press.

An exploration of the ethical responsibilities of authors, texts, and readers. Booth extends and develops many of the concepts first introduced in *The Rhetoric of Fiction*.

The Vocation of a Teacher: Rhetorical Occasions, 1967–1988 (1988) Chicago, IL: University of Chicago Press.

A collection of essays in which Booth celebrates teaching as a vocation.

The Rhetoric of Rhetoric: The Quest for Effective Communication (2004) Blackwell Manifesto Series, Oxford: Blackwell.

Aimed at the general reader, this book provides a brief history of rhetoric, and explores both why it has diminished in importance as a branch of study and why it has once again become popular in academic circles. Booth continues what was a life-long campaign of advocating the central role rhetoric has to play in every element of human experience.

WORKS ON BOOTH

Much of the work on Booth is different from that on James and Trilling in that it consists not just of expositions and commentaries on his concepts and methods, but of attempts to apply, revise, and contest them. Below is a sample of the large amount of material that draws in some way or other on Booth's work.

Antczak, Frederick J. (ed.) (1995) *Rhetoric and Pluralism: Legacies of Wayne Booth*, Columbus, OH: Ohio State University Press.

A collection of essays that surveys the impact of Booth's work.

Baker, John Ross (1977) 'From Imitation to Rhetoric: The Chicago Critics, Wayne C. Booth and *Tom Jones*', in Mark Spilka (ed.) *Towards a Poetics of Fiction*, Bloomington, IN and London: Indiana University Press: 136–56.

Discusses Booth's relation to Aristotle and the Chicago School.

Bialostosky, Don (1985) 'Booth's Rhetoric, Bakhtin's Dialogics, and the Future of Novel Criticism', *Philosophy and Literature* 4: 257–65.

A comparison of Booth and Bakhtin.

Chatman, Seymour (1989) 'The "Rhetoric of Fiction"', in James Phelan (ed.) (1996) *Reading Narrative: Form, Ethics, Ideology*, Columbus, OH: Ohio State University Press: 40–56.

Attacks the catch-all nature of Booth's concept of narrative as rhetoric.

Comstock, Gary (1984) 'Wayne C. Booth, Pluralist', *Religious Studies Review*, 10: 252–7.

Surveys Booth's output within the framework of pluralism and pragmatism.

Kilham, John (1966) 'The "Second Self" in Novel Criticism', *British Journal of Aesthetics*, 6: 272–90.

An article on Booth that Booth himself challenges in '*The Rhetoric of Fiction* and the Poetics of Fiction' (1977) in Mark Spilka (ed.) *Towards a Poetics of Fiction*, Bloomington, IN and London: Indiana University Press.

Phelan, James (1988) 'Wayne C. Booth', *Modern American Critics Since 1955 (Dictionary of Literary Biography* 67), ed. Gregory S. Jay, Detroit, MI: Bruccoli Clark Layman: 49–66.

A comprehensive evaluation of Booth's life and work.

—— (1996) *Narrative as Rhetoric: Technique, Audiences, Ethics, Ideology*, Columbus, OH: Ohio State University Press.

A major re-examination of Booth's key concepts.

Richter, David (1982) 'The Second Flight of the Phoenix: Neo-Aristotelianism Since Crane', *Eighteenth Century*, 23: 27–48.

Sees Booth as a second-generation neo-Aristotelian who is much more interested in interpretation than his predecessors.

Schwartz, Daniel R. (1985) 'Reading as a Moral Activity', *Sewanee Review*, 93: 480–5.

Surveys the continuing relevance of *The Rhetoric of Fiction*.

Stecker, Robert (1987) 'Apparent, Implied, and Postulated Authors', *Philosophy and Literature*, 11: 258–71.

A discussion of Booth's concept of the implied author.

GENERAL

Gibson, Andrew (1996) *Towards a Postmodern Theory of Narrative*, Edinburgh: Edinburgh University Press.

Gibson attacks the whole idea that there can be any such manifestation as 'voice' in narrative.

Graff, Gerald (1987) *Professing Literature*: *An Institutional History*, Chicago, IL and London: University of Chicago Press.

Deals with the institutional context relevant to Trilling and Booth.

Lanser, Susan Sniader (1981) *The Narrative Act*: *The Point of View in Fiction*, Princeton, NJ: Princeton University Press.

An historical-theoretical approach to point of view.

Leitch, Vincent B. (1988) *American Literary Criticism from the Thirties to the Eighties*, New York: Columbia University Press.

Useful on both Trilling and Booth.

McDonald, Walter R. (1969) 'The Inconsistencies in Henry James's Aesthetics', *Texas Studies in Literature and Language*, 10: 585–97.

A broad attack on New Critical appropriations of James.

Peer, Willie van and Seymour Chatman (eds) (2001) *New Perspectives on Narrative Perspective*, Albany, NY: State University of New York Press.

The most recent collection of essays to tackle the concept of point of view. There is both a good history of the concept here and a sense of where it stands at the beginning of the twenty-first century.

Rimmon-Kenan, Shlomith (1983) *Narrative Fiction*: *Contemporary Poetics*, New Accents, London: Methuen.

Not only a good introduction to narratology, but also a synthesis of and reaction to the work of Genette (not least in relation to Booth and James).

WORKS CITED

Note: The following abbreviations are used in references to the Library of America edition of Henry James's work:

LCEL – (1984) *Essays on Literature, American Writers, English Writers. Literary Criticism*, Vol. 1, Library of America, New York: Literary Classics of the United States, Inc.

LCFW – (1984) *French Writers, Other European Writers, The Prefaces to the New York Edition. Literary Criticism*, Vol. 2, Library of America, New York: Literary Classics of the United States, Inc.

Abrams, M. H. (1953) *The Mirror and the Lamp: Romantic Theory and the Critical Tradition*, New York: Oxford University Press.

Allott, Miriam (1959) *Novelists on the Novel*, London: Routledge & Kegan Paul.

Anderson, Quentin, Stephen Donadio, and Steven Marcus (eds) (1977) *Art, Politics, and Will: Essays in Honor of Lionel Trilling*, New York: Basic Books.

Antczak, Frederick J. (ed.) (1995) *Rhetoric and Pluralism: Legacies of Wayne Booth*, Columbus, OH: Ohio State University Press.

Aristotle (1972) *Poetics*, in D. A. Russell and M. Winterbottom (eds) *Ancient Literary Criticism: The Principal Texts in New Translations*, Oxford: Clarendon Press: 85–131.

Arnold, Matthew (1869) *Culture and Anarchy*, J. Dover Wilson (ed.) (1969), Cambridge: Cambridge University Press.

—— (1887) 'Count Leo Tolstoi', in Christopher Ricks (ed.) (1972) *Selected Criticism of Matthew Arnold*, New York and Scarborough, Ontario: Signet: 454–73.

Baker, John Ross (1977) 'From Imitation to Rhetoric: The Chicago Critics, Wayne C. Booth and *Tom Jones*', in Mark Spilka (ed.) *Towards a Poetics of Fiction*, Bloomington, IN and London: Indiana University Press: 136–56.

Bakhtin, Mikhail (1973) *Problems of Dostoevsky's Poetics*, trans. R. W. Rotsel, Ann Arbor, MI: Ardis.

Bal, Mieke (1985) *Narratology: Introduction to the Theory of Narrative*, trans. Christine van Boheemen, Toronto: University of Toronto Press.

Banfield, Ann (1982) *Unspeakable Sentences: Narration and Representation in the Language of Fiction*, London: Routledge & Kegan Paul.

Barbauld, Anna Laetitia (1804) 'A Biographical Account of Samuel Richardson', in Miriam Allott (ed.) (1959) *Novelists on the Novel*, London: Routledge & Kegan Paul: 258–60.

Barthes, Roland (1968) 'The Death of the Author', in Vincent B. Leitch (ed.) (2001) *The Norton Anthology of Theory and Criticism*, New York and London: W. W. Norton & Co.: 1466–70.

Beach, Joseph Warren (1918) *The Method of Henry James* (rev. edn 1954), New Haven, CT: Yale University Press.

—— (1932) *The Twentieth-Century Novel: Studies in Technique*, New York and London: The Century Co.

Besant, Walter (1884) *The Art of Fiction*, Boston, MA: Cupples, Upham and Co.

Bialostosky, Don (1985) 'Booth's Rhetoric, Bakhtin's Dialogics, and the Future of Novel Criticism', *Philosophy and Literature*, 4: 257–65.

Blackmur, Richard P. (ed.) (1934) *The Art of the Novel: Critical Prefaces by Henry James*, New York and London: Charles Scribner's Sons.

Bloom, Alexander (1986) *Prodigal Sons: The New York Intellectuals and Their World*, New York: Oxford University Press.

Booth, Wayne C. (1961) *The Rhetoric of Fiction*, 2nd edn 1983, Chicago, IL: Chicago University Press.

—— (1970) *Now Don't Try to Reason with Me: Essays and Ironies for a Credulous Age*, Chicago, IL: Chicago University Press.

—— (1974a) *Modern Dogma and the Rhetoric of Assent*, Notre Dame: Notre Dame University Press.

—— (1974b) *A Rhetoric of Irony*, Chicago, IL: Chicago University Press.

—— (1978) Rev. of *Teller and Listeners: Narrative Imagination*, by Barbara Hardy, *Modern Language Review*, 73: 144–51.

—— (1979) *Critical Understanding: The Powers and Limits of Pluralism*, Chicago, IL and London: Chicago University Press.

—— (1983a) 'Afterword', *The Rhetoric of Fiction*, 2nd edn, Chicago, IL: Chicago University Press.

—— (1983b) 'Rhetorical Critics Old and New: The Case of Gérard Genette', in Laurence Lerner (ed.) (1983) *Reconstructing Literature*, Oxford: Blackwell: 123–213.

—— (1984) Introduction, Mikhail Bakhtin, *Problems of Dostoyevsky's Poetics*, trans. Caryl Emerson, Manchester: Manchester University Press: xiii–xxviii.

—— (1988a) *The Company We Keep: An Ethics of Fiction*, Berkeley, CA and London: California University Press.

—— (1988b) *The Vocation of a Teacher: Rhetorical Occasions, 1967–1988*, Chicago, IL: University of Chicago Press.

—— (2004) *The Rhetoric of Rhetoric: The Quest for Effective Communication*, Oxford: Blackwell.

Boyers, Robert (1977) *Lionel Trilling: Negative Capability and the Wisdom of Avoidance*, Columbia, MO and London: University of Missouri Press.

Brooks, Cleanth (1947) *The Well Wrought Urn: Studies in the Structure of Poetry*, New York: Reynal & Hitchcock.

—— and Robert Penn Warren (1938) *Understanding Poetry*, New York: Henry Holt.

—— and —— (1943) *Understanding Fiction*, New York: F. S. Crofts & Co.

Brooks, Van Wyck (1925) *The Pilgrimage of Henry James*, New York: E. P. Dutton & Co.

Cervantes Saavedra, Miguel de (1605–15) *Don Quixote* (2003), trans. John Rutherford, Penguin Classics, Harmondsworth: Penguin.

Chace, William M. (1980) *Lionel Trilling*: *Criticism and Politics*, Stanford, CA: Stanford University Press.

Chatman, Seymour (1978) *Story and Discourse*: *Narrative Structure in Fiction and Film*, Ithaca, NY and London: Cornell University Press.

—— (1989) 'The "Rhetoric of Fiction"', in James Phelan (ed.) *Reading Narrative: Form, Ethics, Ideology*, Columbus, OH: Ohio State University Press: 40–56.

Clarke, George (1898) 'The Novel-Reading Habit', in Peter Rawlings (ed.) (2002) *Americans on Fiction, 1776–1900*, 3 vols, London: Pickering & Chatto: 359–66.

Cohn, Dorrit (1978) *Transparent Minds*: *Narrative Modes for Presenting Consciousness in Fiction*, Princeton, NJ: Princeton University Press, 1978.

Coleridge, Samuel Taylor (1817), *Biographia Literaria*, 2 vols, ed. J. Shawcross (1917), Oxford: Oxford University Press.

—— (1811–18) *Coleridge's Lectures and Notes on Shakespere and Other English Poets*, ed. T. Ashe (1914), London: G. Bell & Sons, Ltd.

Compton-Burnett, Ivy (1945) 'A Conversation between I. Compton-Burnett and M. Jourdain', in Miriam Allott (ed.) (1959) *Novelists on the Novel*, London: Routledge & Kegan Paul: 249.

Comstock, Gary (1984) 'Wayne C. Booth, Pluralist', *Religious Studies Review*, 10: 252–7.

Coxe, Arthur Cleveland (1851) 'The Writings of Hawthorne', *Church Review*, 3: 489–511.

Daugherty, Sarah B. (1981) *The Literary Criticism of Henry James*, Athens, OH: Ohio University Press.

Dickstein, Morris (1992) *Double Agent: The Critic and Society*, New York and Oxford: Oxford University Press.

Donoghue, Denis (1955) 'The Critic in Reaction', in John Rodden (ed.) (1999) *Lionel Trilling and the Critics: Opposing Selves*, Lincoln, NE and London: University of Nebraska Press: 215–22.

—— (1978) 'Trilling, Mind, and Society', *Sewanee Review*, 86: 161–86.

Falk, Richard P. (1955) 'The Literary Criticism of the Genteel Decades, 1870–1900', in Floyd Stovall (ed.) *The Development of American Literary Criticism*, New Haven, CT: College and University Press.

Fergusson, Francis (1943) 'James's Idea of Dramatic Form', *Kenyon Review*, 5: 495–507.

Fielding, Henry (1749) *Tom Jones* (1998), Oxford World's Classics, Oxford: Oxford Paperbacks.

Fish, Stanley (1980) *Is there a Text in this Class?: The Authority of Interpretive Communities*, Cambridge, MA and London: Harvard University Press.

Frank, Joseph (1956) 'Lionel Trilling and the Conservative Imagination', *Sewanee Review*, 64: 46–54.

Freedman, Jonathan (1993) 'Trilling, James, and the Uses of Cultural Criticism', *Henry James Review*, 14: 141–50.

French, Phillip (1980) *Three Honest Men: Edmund Wilson, F. R. Leavis, Lionel Trilling: A Critical Mosaic*, Manchester: Carcanet New Press.

Freud, Sigmund (1920) 'Beyond the Pleasure Principle', in *On Metapsychology: The Theory of Psychoanalysis* (1984), Harmondsworth: Penguin: 269–338.

Friedman, Norman (1975) *Form and Meaning in Fiction*, Athens, GA: University of Georgia Press.

Genette, Gérard (1980) *Narrative Discourse: An Essay in Method*, trans. Jane E. Lewin, Ithaca, NY and New York: Cornell University Press.

—— (1988) *Narrative Discourse Revisited*, trans. Jane E. Lewin, Ithaca, NY and New York: Cornell University Press.

Gibson, Andrew (1996) *Towards a Postmodern Theory of Narrative*, Edinburgh: Edinburgh University Press.

Gibson, Walker (1950) 'Authors, Speakers, Readers, and Mock Readers', *College English*, 11, 265–9.

Goode, John (1966) 'The Art of Fiction: Walter Besant and Henry James', in David Howard, John Lucas, and John Goode (eds) *Tradition and Tolerance in Nineteenth-Century Fiction*: *Critical Essays on Some English and American Novels*, London: Routledge & Kegan Paul: 243–81.

Gordon, Caroline (1957) *How to Read a Novel*, New York: Viking Press.

—— and Allen Tate (eds) (1950) *The House of Fiction: An Anthology of the Short Story*, 2nd edn, New York: Charles Scribner's Sons.

Graff, Gerald (1987) *Professing Literature: An Institutional History*, Chicago, IL and London: University of Chicago Press.

Graham, Kenneth (1965) *English Criticism of the Novel, 1865–1900*, Oxford: Clarendon Press.

Hawthorne, Nathaniel (1850) *The Scarlet Letter*, Boston, MA: Ticknor, Reed, and Fields.

Hirsch Jr, E. D. (1960) 'Objective Interpretation', in Vincent B. Leitch (ed.) (2001) *The Norton Anthology of Theory and Criticism*, New York and London: W. W. Norton & Co.: 1684–1709.

—— (1967) *Validity in Interpretation*, New Haven, CT and London: Yale University Press.

Holloway, John (1973) 'Sincerely, Lionel Trilling', in John Rodden (ed.) (1999) *Lionel Trilling and the Critics: Opposing Selves*, Lincoln, NE and London: University of Nebraska Press: 335–42.

Iser, Wolfgang (1974) *The Implied Reader: Patterns of Communication in Prose Fiction from Bunyan to Beckett*, Baltimore, MD and London: Johns Hopkins University Press.

James, Henry (1865) 'Rev. of *Miss Mackenzie*, by Anthony Trollope', *LCEL* 1312–17.

—— (1866a) 'The Novels of George Eliot', *LCEL* 912–33.

—— (1866b) 'Rev. of *The Belton Estate*, by Anthony Trollope', *LCEL* 1322–6.

—— (1867; 1999) Letter to Thomas Sergeant Perry, 20 September 1867, *Henry James: A Life in Letters*, ed. Philip Horne, Harmondsworth: Allen Lane, Penguin: 13–18.

—— (1876) 'The Minor French Novelists', *LCFW* 159–83.

—— (1878) *French Poets and Novelists*, London: Macmillan & Co.

—— (1879; 1984 edn) *Hawthorne*, *LCEL* 315–457.

—— (1880) 'Rev. of *Nana*, by Émile Zola', *LCFW* 864–70.

—— (1881; 2003 edn) *The Portrait of a Lady*, Harmondsworth: Penguin.

—— (1883) 'Anthony Trollope', *LCEL* 1330–54.

—— (1884; 1984 edn) 'The Art of Fiction', *LCEL* 44–65.

—— (1886) *The Princess Casamassima*, London: Macmillan & Co.

—— (1888a) 'Guy de Maupassant', *LCFW* 521–49.

—— (1888b) *Partial Portraits*, London: Macmillan & Co.

—— (1890a) Letter to W. D. Howells, in James E. Miller (ed.) (1972) *Theory of Fiction: Henry James*, Lincoln, NE: University of Nebraska Press: 65–6.

—— (1890b) Letter to William James, 23 July 1890, in Leon Edel (ed.) (1984) *Henry James Letters*, Cambridge, MA: Belknap Press, Harvard University Press: 3: 300–1.

—— (1891) 'The Science of Criticism', *LCEL* 95–9.

—— (1893a) *Essays in London and Elsewhere*, London: James R. Osgood, McIlvaine & Co.

—— (1893b) *Picture and Text*, New York: Harper & Bros.

—— (1894) *Guy Domville*, London: J. Miles & Co. (for private circulation only).

—— (1896a) 'The Figure in the Carpet', in Peter Rawlings (ed.) (1984) *Henry James' Shorter Masterpieces*, 2 vols, Brighton and New Jersey: Harvester Press and Barnes and Noble: 2: 46–88.

—— (1896b) 'Ivan Turgeneff', *LCFW* 1027–34.

—— (1897) 'London Notes', *LCEL* 1387–413.

—— (1898) *The Turn of the Screw*, ed. John McRae (2001), Harmondsworth: Penguin.

—— (1899) 'The Future of the Novel', *LCEL* 100–110.

—— (1900) Letter to H. G. Wells, 29 January 1900, in Leon Edel (ed.) (1984) *Henry James Letters*, Cambridge, MA: Belknap Press, Harvard University Press: 4: 132–3.

—— (1902a) 'Introduction', *Madame Bovary*, by Gustave Flaubert, *LCFW* 314–46.

—— (1902b) *The Wings of the Dove*, John Bayley and Patricia Crick (eds) (1965), Harmondsworth: Penguin.

—— (1903) *The Ambassadors*, ed. Harry Levin (1986), Harmondsworth: Penguin.

—— (1904) *The Golden Bowl* (2001), Harmondsworth: Penguin.

—— (1907–9) Prefaces, *The Novels and Tales of Henry James*, New York Edition, *LCFW* 1035–1341.

—— (1908) Letter to W. D. Howells, 17 August 1908, in Richard P. Blackmur (ed.) (1947) *The Art of the Novel*, New York: Charles Scribner's Sons: viii.

—— (1912) Letter to Hugh Walpole, in Leon Edel (ed.) (1984) *Henry James Letters*, Belknap Press, Cambridge, MA: Harvard University Press: 4: 618–20.

—— (1914) 'The New Novel', in *Notes on Novelists*, London: J. M. Dent & Sons, Ltd: 249–87.

—— (1914) *Notes on Novelists*, London: J. M. Dent & Sons, Ltd.

—— (1915) Letter to H. G. Wells, 10 July 1915, in Leon Edel (ed.) (1984) *Henry James Letters*, Cambridge, MA and London: Belknap Press, Harvard University Press: 3: 768–70.

—— (1987) *The Complete Notebooks of Henry James*, Leon Edel and Lyall H. Powers (eds), New York and Oxford: Oxford University Press.

Jones, Vivien (1984) *James the Critic*, London: Macmillan & Co.

Joyce, James (1916) *The Portrait of the Artist as a Young Man* (1960), Penguin Modern Classics, Harmondsworth: Penguin.

Kafka, Franz (1937) *The Castle* (2000), Penguin Modern Classics, trans. J. Underwood, Harmondsworth: Penguin.

Kearney, Richard (1988) *The Wake of Imagination: Ideas of Creativity in Culture*, London: Hutchinson.

Keats, John (1820) 'Ode on a Grecian Urn', in Cleanth Brooks and Robert Penn Warren (eds) (1938), 4th edn, *Understanding Poetry*, New York: Holt, Rinehart & Winston.

Kilham, John (1966) 'The "Second Self" in Novel Criticism', *British Journal of Aesthetics*, 6: 272–90.

Krupnick, Mark (1986) *Lionel Trilling and the Fate of Cultural Criticism*, Evanston, IL: Northwestern University Press.

Lanser, Susan Sniader (1981) *The Narrative Act: Point of View in Prose Fiction*, Princeton, NJ: Princeton University Press.

Lee, Vernon (1923) *The Handling of Words and Other Studies in Literary Psychology*, ed. David Seed (1992), Lewiston, NY and Lampeter: E. Mellen Press.

Leitch, Vincent B. (1988) *American Literary Criticism from the Thirties to the Eighties*, New York: Columbia University Press.

Locke, John (1690) *An Essay Concerning Human Understanding*, ed. Peter H. Nidditch (1975), Oxford: Clarendon Press.

Lubbock, Percy (1921) *The Craft of Fiction*, London: Jonathan Cape.

McDonald, Walter R. (1969) 'The Inconsistencies in Henry James's Aesthetics', *Texas Studies in Literature and Language*, 10: 585–97.

McWhirter, David (ed.) (1995) *Henry James's New York Edition: The Construction of Authorship*, Stanford, CA: Stanford University Press.

Marsh, Edward (1909) 'Henry James: Auto-Critic', in Peter Rawlings (ed.) (1993) *Critical Essays on Henry James*, Critical Thought Series 5, Aldershot and Brookfield, VT: Scolar Press: 107–11.

Marshall, Adré (1998) *The Turn of the Mind: Constituting Consciousness in Henry James*, London: Associated University Presses.

Martin, Timothy P. (1980) 'Henry James and Percy Lubbock: From Mimesis to Formalism', *Novel*, 14: 20–9.

Matthiessen, F. O. (1944) *Henry James: The Major Phase*, Oxford: Oxford University Press.

Mazzocco, Robert (1965) 'Beyond Criticism', in John Rodden (ed.) (1999) *Lionel Trilling and the Critics: Opposing Selves*, Lincoln, NE and London: University of Nebraska Press: 260–8.

Miller, James E. (ed.) (1972) *Theory of Fiction: Henry James*, Lincoln, NE and London: University of Nebraska Press.

Morrison, Sister Kristin (1961) 'James's and Lubbock's Differing Points of View', *Nineteenth-Century Fiction*, 16: 245–55.

Nietzsche, Friedrich (1883–5) *Thus Spoke Zarathustra*, Modern Library, Walter Arnold Kaufmann (ed.) (1995), New York: Random House.

—— (1886) *Beyond Good and Evil: Prelude to a Philosophy of the Future* (1998), New York: Dover Publications.

—— (1887) 'The Genealogy of Morals: A Polemic', trans. Horace B. Samuel (1910), *The Complete Works of Friedrich Nietzsche*, vol. 13, Edinburgh and London: T. N. Foulis.

Nussbaum, Martha C. (1990) *Love's Knowledge: Essays on Philosophy and Literature*, New York and Oxford: Oxford University Press.

O'Hara, Daniel T. (1988) *Lionel Trilling: The Work of Liberation*, The Wisconsin Project on American Writers, Madison, WI: University of Wisconsin Press.

Parrington, V. L. (1927–30) *Main Currents in American Thought: An Interpretation of American Literature from the Beginnings to 1920*, 3 vols, New York: Harcourt, Brace & Co.

Pater, Walter (1893) *The Renaissance: Studies in Art and Poetry*, ed. Donald L. Hill (1980), Berkeley, CA: University of California Press.

Pearson, John H. (1997) *The Prefaces of Henry James: Framing the Modern Reader*, University Park, PA: Pennsylvania State University Press.

Peer, Willie van and Seymour Chatman (eds) (2001) *New Perspectives on Narrative Perspective*, New York: State University of New York Press.

Peterson, Dale E. (1975) *The Clement Vision: Poetic Realism in Turgenev and James*, Port Washington, NY and London: Kennikat Press.

Phelan, James (1988) 'Wayne C. Booth', in Gregory S. Jay (ed.) *Modern American Critics since 1955 Dictionary of Literary Biography*, Vol. 67, Detroit, MI: Bruccoli Clark Layman: 49–66.

—— (ed.) (1996) *Narrative as Rhetoric: Technique, Audiences, Ethics, Ideology*, Columbus, OH: Ohio State University Press.

Plato (1972) *Republic*, in D. A. Russell and M. Winterbottom (eds) *Poetics, Ancient Literary Criticism: The Principal Texts in New Translations*, Oxford: Clarendon Press: 50–65.

Podhoretz, Norman (1968) *Making It*, London: Jonathan Cape.

—— (1979) *Breaking Ranks: A Political Memoir*, London: Weidenfeld & Nicolson.

Prince, Gerald (1982) *Narratology: The Form and Functioning of Narrative*, Amsterdam: Mouton.

Rabinowitz, Peter J. (1977) 'Truth in Fiction: A Reexamination of Audiences', *Critical Inquiry*, 4: 121–41.

Rahv, Philip (1943) 'The Heiress of all the Ages', *Partisan Review*, 10: 227–47.

—— (1969) *Literature and the Sixth Sense*, Boston, MA: Houghton Mifflin.

Rawlings, Peter (ed.) (1993) *Critical Essays on Henry James*, Critical Thought Series 5, Aldershot and Brookfield, VT: Scolar Press.

—— (2001) 'Trilling Unlionised', *Essays in Criticism*, 51: 276–82.

—— (ed.) (2002) *Americans on Fiction, 1776–1900*, 3 vols, London: Pickering & Chatto.

Reising, Russell J. (1986) *The Unusable Past: Theory and the Study of American Literature*, New Accents, New York and London: Methuen.

Richter, David (1982) 'The Second Flight of the Phoenix: Neo-Aristotelianism Since Crane', *Eighteenth Century*, 23: 27–48.

Rimmon-Kenan, Shlomith (1983) *Narrative Fiction: Contemporary Poetics*, New Accents, New York and London: Methuen.

Robbe-Grillet, Alain (1957) *Jealousy*, trans. Richard Howard (1959), London: John Calder.

Robert, Marthe (1980) *Origins of the Novel*, in Michael McKeon (ed.) (2000) *Theory of the Novel: A Historical Approach*, Baltimore, MD and London: Johns Hopkins University Press.

Rodden, John (ed.) (1999) *Lionel Trilling and the Critics: Opposing Selves*, Lincoln, NE and London: University of Nebraska Press.

Ross, D. (1976) 'Who's Talking? How Characters become Narrators in Fiction', *Modern Language Notes*, 91: 1222–42.

Rowe, John Carlos (1984) *The Theoretical Dimensions of Henry James*, Madison, WI: University of Wisconsin Press.

—— (1998) *The Other Henry James*, New Americanists, Durham, NC and London: Duke University Press.

Sacks, Sheldon (1964) *Fiction and the Shape of Belief: A Study of Henry Fielding, with Glances at Swift, Johnson and Richardson*, Berkeley and Los Angeles, CA: University of California Press.

Said, Edward (1993) *Culture and Imperialism*, London: Chatto & Windus.

Sale, Roger (1973) 'Lionel Trilling', in John Rodden (ed.) (1999) *Lionel Trilling and the Critics: Opposing Selves*, Lincoln, NE and London: University of Nebraska Press: 327–34.

Scholes, Robert (1973) 'The Illiberal Imagination', *New Literary History*, 4: 521–40.

Schuyler, Montgomery (1908) 'Henry James Done Over', in Peter Rawlings (ed.) (1993) *Critical Essays on Henry James*, Critical Thought Series 5, Aldershot and Brookfield, VT: Scolar Press: 102–6.

Schwartz, Daniel R. (1985) 'Reading as a Moral Activity', *Sewanee Review*, 93: 480–5.

Schwartz, Delmore (1953) 'The Duchess' Red Shoes', *Partisan Review*, 20: 55–73.

Scott, Nathan A. (1973) *Three American Moralists: Mailer, Bellow, Trilling*, Notre Dame and London: University of Notre Dame Press.

Seed, David (1981) 'The Narrator in James's Criticism', *Philological Quarterly*, 60: 501–21.

Shoben, Edward J. (1981) *Lionel Trilling*, New York: Frederick Ungar.

Simpson, Lewis P. (1987) 'Lionel Trilling and the Agency of Terror', in John Rodden (ed.) (1999) *Lionel Trilling and the Critics: Opposing Selves*, Lincoln, NE and London: University of Nebraska Press: 404–20.

Spilka, Mark (1977) 'Henry James and Walter Besant: "The Art of Fiction"' Controversy', in Mark Spilka (ed.) *Towards a Poetics of Fiction*, Bloomington, IN and London: Indiana University Press: 190–208.

Stecker, Robert (1987) 'Apparent, Implied, and Postulated Authors', *Philosophy and Literature*, 11: 258–71.

Stevenson, Robert Louis (1884) 'A Humble Remonstrance', in Saxe Commins (ed.) (1947) *Selected Writings of Robert Louis Stevenson*, New York: Random House: 915–25.

Tanner, Stephen L. (1988) *Lionel Trilling*, Twayne's United States Authors Series, Boston, MA: Twayne Publishers.

Teres, Harvey M. (1996) *Renewing the Left: Politics, Imagination, and the New York Intellectuals*, New York and Oxford: Oxford University Press.

Tilford Jr, John E. (1958) 'James the Old Intruder', *Modern Fiction Studies*, 4: 157–64.

Trilling, Lionel (1939) *Matthew Arnold*, New York: W. W. Norton & Co.

—— (1943a) 'Of This Time, of That Place', in *Of This Time, of That Place and Other Stories*, Uniform Edition (1979), New York and London: Harcourt Brace Jovanovich: 72–116.

—— (1943b) *E. M. Forster*, 2nd edn, New York: New Directions.

—— (1947) *The Middle of the Journey*, New York: Viking.

—— (1950) *The Liberal Imagination: Essays on Literature and Society*, Uniform Edition (1978), New York and London: Harcourt Brace Jovanovich.

—— (1955a) *Freud and the Crisis of Our Culture*, Boston, MA: Beacon Press.

—— (1955b) *The Opposing Self: Nine Essays in Criticism*, Uniform Edition (1978), New York and London: Harcourt Brace Jovanovich.

—— (1956) *A Gathering of Fugitives*, Boston, MA: Beacon.

—— (1957) 'The Person of the Artist', in Diana Trilling (ed.) (1982) *Speaking of Literature and Society*, New York and London: Harcourt Brace Jovanovich: 285–94.

—— (1958) 'The Last Lover', in Diana Trilling (ed.) (1982) *Speaking of Literature and Society*, New York and London: Harcourt Brace Jovanovich: 322–42.

—— (1965) *Beyond Culture*: *Essays on Literature and Learning*, New York: Viking.

—— (1967) 'Enemies', in Diana Trilling (ed.) (1981) *Prefaces to the Experience of Literature*, New York and London: Harcourt Brace Jovanovich: 96–101.

—— (1968) 'On Irony: An Addendum', in Diana Trilling (ed.) (1982) *Speaking of Literature and Society*, New York and London: Harcourt Brace Jovanovich: 407–9.

—— (1970) 'Introduction: What is Criticism?' in Lionel Trilling (ed.) *Literary Criticism*: *An Introductory Reader*, New York: Holt, Rinehart & Winston, Inc.: 1–28.

—— (1971) 'Some Notes for an Autobiographical Lecture', in Diana Trilling (ed.) (1979) *Lionel Trilling*: *The Last Decade*: *Essays and Reviews, 1965–75*, New York and London: Harcourt Brace Jovanovich: 226–41.

—— (1972) *Sincerity and Authenticity*, Cambridge, MA: Harvard University Press.

—— (1973) *Mind in the Modern World*, New York: Viking.

—— (1979a) *The Last Decade: Essays and Review, 1965–7*, Diana Trilling (ed.), New York and London: Harcourt Brace Jovanovich.

—— (1979b) *Of This Time, of That Place and Other Stories*, New York and London: Harcourt Brace Jovanovich.

—— (1982) *Speaking of Literature and Society*, Diana Trilling (ed.) New York and London: Harcourt Brace Jovanovich.

—— (2000) *The Moral Obligation to be Intelligent*: *Selected Essays*, Leon Wieseltier (ed.), Leon, NY: Farrar, Strauss, & Giroux.

Uspensky, Boris (1973) *A Poetics of Composition: The Structure of the Artistic Text and Typology of a Compositional Form*, trans. V. Zavarin and S. Wittig, Berkeley, CA: University of California Press.

Van Ghent, Dorothy (1953) *The English Novel: Form and Function*, Harper Torch Books, New York: Rinehart.

Walker, Pierre A. (ed.) (1999) *Henry James on Culture: Collected Essays on Politics and the American Social Scene*, Lincoln, NE and London: University of Nebraska Press.

Ward, J. A. (1967) *The Search for Form: Studies in the Structure of James's Fiction*, Chapel Hill, NC: University of North Carolina Press.

Weimann, Robert (1984) *Structure and Society in Literary History: Studies in the History and Theory of Historical Criticism*, expanded edn, Baltimore, MD and London: Johns Hopkins University Press.

Wellek, René (1965) 'Henry James', *A History of Modern Criticism: 1750–1950*, vol. 4, *The Later Nineteenth Century*, London: Jonathan Cape: 213–37.

—— (1986) 'Lionel Trilling', in his *A History of Modern Criticism*, vol. 6, *American Criticism, 1900–1950*, New Haven, CT and London: Yale University Press: 123–43.

Wieseltier, Leon (2000) 'Introduction' to Lionel Trilling, *The Moral Obligation to be Intelligent: Selected Essays*, New York: Farrar, Strauss, and Giroux: ix–xvii.

Wimsatt, W. K. and Monroe C. Beardsley (1946) 'The Intentional Fallacy', in Vincent B. Leitch (ed.) (2001) *The Norton Anthology of Theory and Criticism*, New York and London: W. W. Norton & Co.: 1374–87.

—— (1949) 'The Affective Fallacy', in Vincent B. Leitch (ed.) *The Norton Anthology of Theory and Criticism*, New York and London: W. W. Norton & Co.: 1387–1403.

Zinn, Christopher (1984) 'From the Notebooks of Lionel Trilling', *Partisan Review*, 51: 496–515.

INDEX

Boyers, Robert 138
Brooks, Cleanth 91, 121
Brooks, Van Wyck 120
Butor, Michel 35

career author 15–16, 64; *see also* narrative
centres of consciousness 2, 16, 17, 71–86, 98, 120, 122: definition of 77; *see also* Beach; Chatman; consciousness; Friedman; Genette; Gordon; Lubbock; pluralism; point of view
Chace, William M. 138
Chatman, Seymour 127–8, 142, 144
Chekhov, Anton 69
Chicago School 12–14, 63–4, 68: and Aristotle 13, 63–4; principal ideas of 14; *see also* pluralism
civil rights 10
Clarke, George 2
coduction 114–15: definition of 115; *see also* reader
Cohn, Dorrit 123, 134
Coleridge, Samuel Taylor 2, 25
communication 12–13, 14, 15–16, 17, 18, 24, 33, 55, 72, 87, 89–92, 117: model of 16; and reading process, five models of 89–92; *see also* Booth; narrative; novel
communism 8, 9–10, 120; *see also* Marxism
Company We Keep, The (Booth) 12, 15–16, 16–17, 33, 43, 64, 65, 87, 94, 101, 102, 113, 114, 115, 116–17, 125, 127, 141
Compton-Burnett, Ivy 44
Comstock, Gary 143
connotation: definition of 48; *see also* denotation

Conrad, Joseph 52, 59, 80, 110, 128
consciousness 2, 16, 17, 45, 55, 57, 77, 78, 79, 80, 81, 82–6, 98, 105–8, 106, 107, 110, 112, 113, 116, 117, 120, 123, 134: definition of 83; and moral consciousness 83, 105–8, 107, 110, 112, 113, 116; *see also* centres of consciousness; pluralism; point of view
constructed influence 72: definition of 72
counter-culture; *see* culture
Crane, R. S. 12, 13, 29, 143
Crane, Stephen 29
Critical Understanding (Booth) 13, 32–3, 84–5, 87–9, 95, 98, 100–2, 140
culture 4, 8, 10, 12, 44–5, 46, 47, 49, 54, 72, 100, 101, 104, 109, 112–13, 114, 116, 117, 122, 125: Arnold on 45; counter-culture 10, 12, 122; definition of, 45; Trilling's definition of 45

Daugherty, Sarah B. 133
death instinct 50: definition of 50; *see also* Freud
denotation 48, 50: definition of 48; *see also* connotation
descriptive criticism 37: definition of 37; *see also* normative criticism
Dickens, Charles 2, 47, 48, 52–3
Dickstein, Morris 138
Diderot, Denis 110
diegesis 51, 53: definition of 51; *see also* mimesis, narrative
discourse 127–8: definition of 128; *see also* Chatman; Genette; story

Hegel, Georg Wilhelm Friedrich 108

Hirsch, E. D. 101

Hoggart, Richard 137

Homer 51

Howells, William Dean 41, 47, 48–9

impersonality 34, 51, 60–3, 65–6, 69, 78–9: definition of 34; Flaubert on 34, 35, 65

implied author 2, 15–16, 58, 59, 63–8, 70, 73, 80, 90, 96, 101, 102–3, 113, 114–15, 124, 129, 142: definition of 64; and flesh-and-blood author 114–15; *see also* narrative; reader

implied reader *see* reader

indolence 50

intentional fallacy 2

interpretation 87–104; *see also* narrative; reader

irony 67, 68, 141: definition of 68; *see also* dramatic irony

Iser, Wolfgang 91, 95

James, Henry: and appreciation 43, 98–100; on artistic sense 106–8; on author's voice 56; on centres of consciousness 2, 17, 71–86, 98, 120, 122; on Conrad 80; and consciousness 2, 16, 17, 55, 77, 78, 79, 80, 81, 82–6, 106, 107, 116, 123; on distance 47; and dramatic narrative 80–2; on ficelles 81–2; and impersonality 65, 78–9; and implied authors 65, 80; on importance of the novel 21–2, 32; on kinds 36, 81–2; legacy of 1–3, 119–30; life and context 3–7; and moral consciousness 105–8, 110, 112,

116; on moral sense 106–8; on morality and the novel 25–6; on narrative commentary 79–80, 81, 82; on omniscience 75, 80, 84; and organic form 23–6, 27, 38, 42, 76, 124, 135; on point of view 73–86, 120; on readers, reading, and interpretation 44, 87–104; on realism and representation 21–2, 39–44; on scene 34, 42, 56, 60–3; on summary 34, 42, 56, 60–3; on 'test of execution' 26, 93, 96; writings of: *Ambassadors, The* 60, 74, 77, 85, 109, 125; *American, The* 43, 78, 84, 85; 'Anthony Trollope' 40, 41, 42, 62; 'Art of Fiction, The' 6, 16, 21–6, 32, 36, 38, 39, 76, 82, 87, 89, 92, 93, 96, 97, 105–8, 121, 129; *Awkward Age, The* 80, 81; *Essays in London and Elsewhere* 5, 132; 'Figure in the Carpet, The' 99; *French Poets and Novelists* 5, 7; *Golden Bowl, The* 1, 77; 'Guy de Maupassant' 65; *Guy Domville* 5; *Hawthorne* 5; Letter to H. G. Wells (1900) 93; Letter to Hugh Walpole (1912) 76; Letter to Thomas Sergeant Perry (1867) 105; Letter to William James (1890) 94; 'London Notes' 56; 'New Novel, The' 42–3, 80; *Notes on Novelists* 5, 132; 'Novels of George Eliot, The' 95; *Partial Portraits* 5; *Portrait of a Lady, The* 1; Prefaces to the New York Edition of the Novels and Tales of Henry James 1, 2, 4, 16, 24, 34, 38, 39–44, 54, 56, 58, 60, 61, 71, 72, 73, 74–86, 87, 93, 94, 97, 98, 102, 106, 107, 109, 121,

realism, definition of 109; and
moral sense 26, 106–8; and novel
6–7, 25–6, 29; pragmatic,
definition of 116; relative,
definition of 116; *see also*
consciousness; Erskine; ethics;
Forster; Nabokov; Puritanism
Mormons 11: definition of 11; *see
also* Smith; Young
Morrison, Sister Kristin 134

Nabokov, Vladimir 112–13, 115,
117; *see also Lolita*
narratee 15–16; *see also* narrative
narrative commentary *see* narrative
narrative: and author 15–16, 55–70,
95–104; and authorial audience,
definition of 100; and authorial
and narrative audiences 16,
100–1, 103, 126–7; and author's
image 15–16; and career author
15–16, 64; and commentary 34,
35, 50, 63, 51, 52, 56, 60–3,
65, 78–80, 81, 82; and
communication 2, 4, 15–16,
32–3, 36–7, 38, 50, 53, 54, 55,
59, 63–6, 69, 70, 85, 99, 95,
112–14, 117, 122, 123, 126,
128; and diegesis 51–3; and
drama 80–2; and ficelles 82; and
flesh-and-blood author 15–16,
101, 126; and flesh-and-blood
reader 15–16, 64, 114–15; and
focalization 78; and interpretation
87–104; and mimesis 88–9; and
narratee 15–16; and narrative
audience, definition of 100; and
narrator 15–16, 55–70, 95–104;
and reader 16, 87–104; and
reading process, five models of
the 89–92; and society 15–16;
and voice 78; *see also* Abrams;

Conrad; distance; Genette;
implied author; kinds; mere
observer; narrative commentary;
narrator; narrator-agent; novel;
omniscience; privilege; reader;
scene; summary; Turgenev
narrator: definition of reliability 68;
and *Lolita* (Nabokov) 112–13;
reliability of 66–70, 112–14
narrator-agent 58–60, 76: definition
of 60; *see also* mere observer
New Criticism 1, 10–11, 13, 71–3,
91, 99–100, 120: definition of 2;
and textual autonomy 97–8
'New Novel, The' (James) 42–3,
80, 132
New York Intellectuals 8, 10, 138,
140
Nietzsche, Friedrich 31, 84, 108,
110, 111: on ethics 108; on will
31
normative criticism: definition of
37; *see also* descriptive criticism
norms: definition of 59
Norris, Frank 29
Notes on Novelists (James) 5, 132
nouveau roman: definition of 35
novel 21–38: and communication
15–16; definition of 22; and
family romance (Freud) 125–6;
judgement of 114–17; and
morality 3, 6–7, 25–6, 29; status
of 2–3, 21–2; *see also* form;
narrative; organic form
'Novels of George Eliot, The'
(James) 95
Now Don't Try to Reason with Me
(Booth) 12, 140
Nussbaum, Martha C. 124–5, 134

'Of This Time, of That Place'
(Trilling) 7

Wells, H. G. 23, 93
What Maisie Knew (James) 60, 79, 124
will 31: definition of 31; and the novel 31; *see also* Nietzsche
Wimsatt, W. K. 2
Wings of the Dove, The 1, 34, 56, 68, 78, 126

Woolf, Virginia 40
Wordsworth, William 22

Young, Brigham 11; *see also* Mormons; Smith

Zinn, Christopher 8
Zola, Émile 5, 40, 41, 42, 123, 132

Related series from Routledge

The New Critical Idiom

Series Editor: John Drakakis, University of Stirling

The New Critical Idiom is an invaluable series of introductory guides to today's critical terminology. Each book:

■ provides a handy, explanatory guide to the use (and abuse) of the term

■ offers an original and distinctive overview by a leading literary and cultural critic

■ relates the term to the larger field of cultural representation

With a strong emphasis on clarity, lively debate and the widest possible breadth of examples, *The New Critical Idiom* is an indispensable approach to key topics in literary studies.

'Easily the most informative and wide-ranging series of its kind, so packed with bright ideas that it has become an indispensable resource for students of literature.'

Terry Eagleton, University of Manchester

A selection of titles available in this series are:

The Author by Andrew Bennett   *Myth* by Laurence Coupe
Comedy by Andrew Stott   *Narrative* by Paul Cobley
Crime Fiction by John Scaggs   *Realism* by Pam Morris
Genre by John Frow   *Romanticism* by Aidan Day
Literature by Peter Widdowson   *Science Fiction* by Adam Roberts

For further information on individual books in
the series and a full range of titles, visit:
www.routledge.com/literature/nci

Related titles from Routledge

The Routledge Dictionary of Literary Terms

Peter Childs and Roger Fowler

The Routledge Dictionary of Literary Terms is a twenty-first century
update of Roger Fowler's seminal *Dictionary of Modern Critical Terms*.
Bringing together original entries written by such celebrated theorists
as Terry Eagleton and Malcolm Bradbury with new definitions of
current terms and controversies, this is the essential reference book
for students of literature at all levels. This book includes:

- New definitions of contemporary critical issues such as
  'Cybercriticism' and 'Globalization'.
- An exhaustive range of entries, covering numerous aspects to
  such topics as genre, form, cultural theory and literary technique.
- Complete coverage of traditional and radical approaches to the
  study and production of literature.
- Thorough account of critical terminology and analyses of key
  academic debates.
- Full cross-referencing throughout and suggestions for further
  reading.

ISBN10: 0–415–36117–6 (hbk)
ISBN10: 0–415–34017–9 (pbk)

ISBN13: 978–0–415–36117–0 (hbk)
ISBN13: 978–0–415–34017–5 (pbk)

Available at all good bookshops
For ordering and further information please visit
www.routledge.com

Related titles from Routledge

Literary Theory: The Basics
Hans Bertens

Part of the successful *Basics* series, this accessible guide provides the ideal first step in understanding literary theory. Hans Bertens:

- leads students through the major approaches to literature which are signalled by the term 'literary theory'
- places each critical movement in its historical (and often political) context
- illustrates theory in practice with examples from much-read texts
- suggests further reading for different critical approaches
- shows that theory can make sense and that it can radically change the way we read.

Covering the basics and much more, this is the ideal book for anyone interested in how we read and why that matters.

ISBN10: 0–415–35112–X (pbk)

ISBN13: 978–0–415–35112–6 (pbk)

Available at all good bookshops
For ordering and further information please visit
www.routledge.com

Related titles from Routledge

Doing English
A Guide for Literature Students
Robert Eaglestone

'*Doing English* . . . is excellent: a thought-provoking and accessible argument exploring the changing character of English Literature as it has developed outside the school curriculum over the last half century.' – *The English and Media Magazine*

'If students read what Eaglestone has to say, they will certainly be more confident in confronting some of the challenges and contradictions which exist in literary studies in universities.' – *Dr Roy Johnson, Mantex.co.uk*

Aimed at students in the final year of secondary education or beginning degrees, this readable book provides the ideal introduction to studying English literature. *Doing English*:

- explains what 'doing English' really means
- introduces current ideas about literature, contexts and interpretations
- bridges the gap between 'traditional' and 'theoretical' approaches to literature, showing why English has had to change and what those changes mean for students of the subject.

Doing English deals with the exciting new ideas and contentious debates that make up English today, covering a broad range of issues from the history of literary studies and the canon to Shakespeare, politics and the future of English. The second edition has been revised throughout and includes a new chapter on narrative. Robert Eaglestone's refreshingly clear explanations and advice make this volume essential reading for all those planning to 'do English' at advanced or degree level.

ISBN10: 0–415–28422–8 (hbk)
ISBN10: 0–415–28423–6 (pbk)

ISBN13: 978–0–415–28422–6 (hbk)
ISBN13: 978–0–415–28423–3 (pbk)

Available at all good bookshops
For further information on our literature series, please visit
www.routledge.com/literature/series.asp

For ordering and further information please visit:
www.routledge.com

Related titles from Routledge

The Routledge Companion to Critical Theory

Simon Malpas and Paul Wake

Routledge Companion of Critical Theory is an indispensable guide for anyone coming to this exciting field of study for the first time.

Exploring ideas from a diverse range of disciplines, this clearly presented text encourages the reader to develop a deeper understanding of how to approach the written word. Defining what is generically referred to as 'critical theory', *Routledge Companion of Critical Theory* explores some of the most complex and fundamental concepts in the field, ranging from historicism to postmodernism, from psychoanalytic criticism to race and postcolonialism.

Key features include:

■ clear and detailed introductory chapters written by experts in each area
■ almost 200 fully cross-referenced dictionary entries
■ a range of illustrations drawn from literature, film and contemporary culture, which illustrate complex theoretical ideas
■ a dictionary of terms and thinkers that students are likely to encounter
■ guidance on further reading to direct students towards crucial primary essays and introductory chapters on each concept.

Tailored to meet the needs of undergraduate students when they first encounter theory, as well as when their knowledge and experience develop and they want to know where to go next, this is the ideal resource for those studying this fascinating area.

ISBN10: 0–415–33295–8 (hbk)
ISBN10: 0–415–33296–6 (pbk)

ISBN13: 978–0–415–33295–8 (hbk)
ISBN13: 978–0–415–33296–5 (pbk)

Available at all good bookshops
For further information on our literature series, please visit
www.routledge.com/literature/series.asp

For ordering and further information please visit:
www.routledge.com

Related titles from Routledge

Critical Practice (Second Edition)
Catherine Belsey

New Accents Series

'A fine assessment of recent work in literary theory and a
suggestive account of new directions for criticism to take.'
William E. Cain

What is poststructuralist theory, and what difference does it make to
literary criticism? Where do we find the meaning of the text: in the
author's head? in the reader's? Or do we, instead, *make* the meaning
in the practice of reading itself? If so, what part do our own values
play in the process of interpretation? And what is the role of the text?

Catherine Belsey explains these and other questions concerning the
relations between human beings and language, readers and texts,
writing and cultural politics. The volume simply and lucidly explains
the views of such key figures as Louis Althusser, Roland Barthes,
Jacques Lacan and Jacques Derrida, and shows their theories at work
in readings of familiar literary texts.

With a new chapter, updated guidance on further reading and
revisions throughout, this second edition of *Critical Practice* is the
ideal guide to the present and the future of literary studies.

ISBN10: 0–415–28005–2 (hbk)
ISBN10: 0–415–28006–0 (pbk)

ISBN13: 978–0–415–28005–1 (hbk)
ISBN13: 978–0–415–28006–0 (pbk)

Available at all good bookshops
For ordering and further information please visit:
www.routledge.com

Related titles from Routledge

The Singularity of Literature
Derek Attridge

'Wonderfully original and challenging.'
J. Hillis Miller

Literature and the literary have proved singularly resistant to definition. Derek Attridge argues that such resistance represents not a dead end, but a crucial starting point from which to explore anew the power and practices of Western art.

In this lively, original volume, the author:

- Considers the implications of regarding the literary work as an innovative cultural event
- Provides a rich new vocabulary for discussions of literature, rethinking such terms as invention, singularity, otherness, alterity, performance and form
- Argues the ethical importance of the literary institution to a culture
- Demonstrates how a new understanding of the literary might be put to work in a "responsible", creative mode of reading

The Singularity of Literature is not only a major contribution to the theory of literature, but also a celebration of the extraordinary pleasure of the literary, for reader, writer, student or critic.

ISBN10: 0–415–33592–2 (hbk)
ISBN10: 0–415–33593–0 (pbk)

ISBN13: 978–0–415–33592–8 (hbk)
ISBN13: 978–0–415–33593–5 (pbk)

Available at all good bookshops
For ordering and further information please visit:
www.routledge.com